GOD, YOU SAID...

"REMINDING GOD OF HIS WORD ON YOUR ENTREPRENEURIAL JOURNEY"

Min. James L. Standfield
"The Authority On Biblical Entrepreneurship"

authorHOUSE

AuthorHouse™
1663 Liberty Drive
Bloomington, IN 47403
www.authorhouse.com
Phone: 833-262-8899

Published by AuthorHouse 05/18/2023

ISBN: 978-1-4389-7105-6 (sc)
ISBN: 978-1-4389-8711-8 (e)

Scripture quotations marked NKJV are taken from the New King James Version. Copyright © 1982 by Thomas Nelson, Inc. Used by permission. All rights reserved.

Print information available on the last page.

Any people depicted in stock imagery provided by Getty Images are models, and such images are being used for illustrative purposes only. Certain stock imagery © Getty Images.

This book is printed on acid-free paper.

CONTENTS

ACKNOWLEDGMENTS

I would like to say thank you to my lovely wife, Monica, who left Corporate America to stand by my side. I could not have gotten any of this done without your help. I also want to say thank you for our three wonderful kids, Thaddeus (8), Gabrielle (7), and Michaela (6). I thank God everyday for you. My success is your success. I love you!

PREFACE

God had prompted me to put together this book sometime in late 2005 as I was teaching a class called "How To Start & Succeed In Business" at the church I currently attend, Evangel Cathedral which is located in Upper Marlboro, Md where Dr. Don Meares is the Bishop and Senior Pastor.

Growing up in Washington, D.C., I never thought about writing a book, I never thought about owning five companies, I never thought about being a motivational speaker, I never thought about being a part of a prison ministry, I never thought about being a teacher at my church, teaching Christian Entrepreneur's how to be successful in their businesses by standing on God's unchanging word. Growing up, all I thought about was playing basketball & having fun. Now here I am, years later, sitting down and putting together a book for the Christian Entrepreneur. Glory be to God.

Anyway, to be a successful Christian Entrepreneur and remain a successful Christian Entrepreneur, the believer, the child of God, the called out one, has to feed on God's word and then remind God of His word. The scriptures teach that the word of God is "living and powerful and sharper than any two edged sword, the word also teaches that God's word shall accomplish what He please, and it shall prosper in the thing for which it was sent. I realize that at any given time, the Christian Entrepreneur can give up and call it quits, because of the pressures of the world. But I have come to know that I am called to be a Christian Entrepreneur and have been called by God Himself to strengthen the

Christian Entrepreneurs in the body of Christ. God said if you delight yourself in Him, that He would give you the desires of your heart. Believer, Christian Entrepreneur, you are called to be great, you are called to changed the world, you are called to be the salt of the earth and the light of the world, you are called to change the marketplace and finally, you are called to change the commonwealth of the world. I trust and pray that you will be blessed by reading this book and that your business will go to another level. God Bless You.

Introduction

GOD IS DRAWN TO MOVEMENT

There are, broadly speaking, two distinct schools of thinking among charismatic Believers with regard to divine guidance and the discovery of God's will for our lives. School one, and by far the largest, is summed up by the mentality that says: 'I don't move without God's guidance'. School two is the complete opposite. It says: 'I don't expect God's guidance until I move.' I wonder which one you are in. Do you believe that God's guidance is the cause of your movement, or an effect your movement causes?

School one adherents believe that divine guidance is like a map showing them where to go and what to do. Whereas, school two followers know that God doesn't do maps, just compasses. That compass is the built-in guidance system God has placed within every Christian Entrepreneur, consisting of their gifts, passions, leanings and deepest concerns. These inner guides are indicators of the way towards their personal 'true north'. School two believers believe that if they follow their heart they will bump into the perfect will of God for their lives without trying to plot a precise course towards it.

Abraham

Abraham was a member of school two. In Hebrews 11 we read that Abraham 'obeyed and went, but he did not know where he was going' *(Hebrews 11:8)*. In other words, Abraham wasn't given a map, just a command to leave where he was and go in the general direction of Canaan. Of course we know that God directed his life at times very specifically, but that was only after he created the initial movement and momentum by his original obedience.

Although Abraham didn't know where he was going, he did know where to leave. God told him to leave his country, people and family. If all you know is that you can't stay where you are, then that's enough to create movement in the right direction. We don't need to know where to go or what to do next before we move. Knowing that you can't stay where you are is your inner compass pulling you towards the future; listen to it and follow it.

God will be many things to your life - a father, provider, healer and restorer - but one thing God will not be is your chauffer. God doesn't want to be your driver in life, He wants you to drive and He will give directions as and when necessary. He wants to edit your life not create it.

I'm a fully paid up member of the second school of guidance! I firmly believe that the bible contains far more evidence to support the idea that God is drawn to people in motion than He is to people who are parked up praying about his will.

WWJD

Remember those 'What Would Jesus Do' bracelets? I think they were probably invented by the first school of guidance; those who don't move before they know they have God's specific guidance. This WWJD fraternity did nothing to help mobilize a church that was already parked up, waiting on God. If our thinking and church cultures become dominated by 'What Would Jesus Do' instead of 'How Would Jesus Think', then we can end up wasting years praying and asking the Lord, 'is it A or B?' When you know how Jesus thinks you will always know what Jesus would do. But when you don't know God's mind, you will start looking for God's Word - often in a random prophecy, directional counsel or word of knowledge from some passing ministry.

Many of you reading this think that God is looking for accuracy and precision from you but I promise you, He isn't. You are not a cruise missile with pre-set coordinates; God doesn't want to point and shoot you. His will is not a tightrope, it's a broad road and once you're travelling on it, God can steer you. God is simply looking for obedience from you, which is worked out by you pointing your life in the general direction of what you already understand to be God's nature and purpose to be.

Take a Step

Consider these often quoted scriptures on the theme of divine guidance:

"In his heart a man plans his course, but the Lord determines his steps" *(Proverbs 16:9)*

"A man's steps are directed by the Lord" *(Proverbs 20:24)*

"The steps of a good man are ordered by the Lord" *(Psalm 37:24)*

These and others we could quote, all indicate that God directs steps or movement not stationary things. *God is drawn to people in motion.*

I remember when Monica and I were on vacation with the kids at the Kennedy Space Center in Cape Canaveral, Florida, one of the engineers telling me that the space shuttle's guidance system wasn't actually engaged or used until it was miles from the ground. Only when it was in full motion, heading in the general direction of space – which is 'up' - did its guidance system kick in. Many of God's people are stuck on the launch pad waiting for guidance to kick in when they already know the general direction is 'up'. Just head 'up'; just get moving in the general non-specific, non-detailed direction of where you know your 'up' is. If you want God's guidance in your life take a step, do something; anything that points you in the direction of God's general will for mankind will do for starters. Step out, attempt something, take a risk, live a little.

If we ever needed a clue as to why what is perhaps the most supernatural book in the Bible, is so supernatural, you need look no further than its title. It is called the book of Acts, not intentions but acts. In it we see a church in motion, a mobile church reaching a lost world. Acts is full of divine guidance, supernatural intervention, angelic jailbreaks and phenomenal miracles. And many churches today are praying for those days to return. But without a commitment to go, move, progress, evangelize or change the marketplace, there's nothing for God to partner with. Acts is a record of the 'steps' of the early church attempting to obey the simple command of Christ to be witnesses to their generation.

Jonathan's perhaps

In 1 Samuel 14 we read the story of Jonathan, King Saul's son, and his armour bearer. At that time Israel was in trouble, suffering at the hands of Saul's poor leadership and under Philistine oppression. As a result they had fled into hiding and Saul was left with just 600 soldiers who had only two swords between them. Saul, the troops and the priest were all gathered for the night around a pomegranate tree. During the early hours of the morning Jonathan woke up his young armour bearer with a ridiculous idea: 'Why don't you and me go and pick a fight with the Philistines?' As if that wasn't crazy enough, the next line was really scary. He said, 'and perhaps the Lord will help us' *(1 Samuel 14:6)*. If I had been the young armour bearer, I think I would have said something like 'Jonathan, are you nuts! There are only two of us and only you have a sword. I've got a better idea, why don't you wake me up when you're sure God will help us!'

However, the Bible records that the young lad in effect replied 'Lets go for it, I'm totally with you!' These two members of the second school of guidance – that is, they didn't expect God's guidance until they moved - were about to change history. Their initiative, their attempt to just do something for God, with no guarantee of personal success seemed to get God's attention. Having said that, God still waited until they had killed 20 Philistines before He got involved by sending a mini earthquake to create a panic. The rest is history. The Philistines were defeated with a little belated help from Saul and the other 600 members of the first school of guidance who were still under the tree, seeking God's will.

God was drawn to Jonathan because he was the only one doing anything. All Jonathan knew was that God was against the Philistines and so he figured that if he pointed his life in the same direction as God and took some steps, maybe God would see and assist that. He was right! Many of God's people are more like Saul, parked up, seeking guidance, while a few others are just attempting something, believing that if it's in line with Gods nature and values that that's enough of a welcome sign for God to get involved. Jonathans question wasn't so much 'what's Gods will in this situation', but more 'how can I give my life in the direction of Gods will?'

You've got to embrace Naomi to meet Boaz

We all remember the story of Ruth, her being redeemed by Boaz and ultimately finishing up in Christ's genealogy as recorded in Matthew chapter one. But what we can easily forget is that Ruth's first appearance in church history wasn't her marriage to Boaz but her embracing of Naomi.

The day that Ruth chose to stick with her aged, poor, bereaved and emotionally empty mother-in-law, she had never heard of Boaz – Ruth simply did what she felt was right. She felt it was right to stand by Naomi and expressed that in what are some of the most powerful words of covenant recorded in scripture: "Where you go I will go, and where you stay I will stay. Your people will be my people and your God my God. Where you die I will die, and there I will be buried. May the LORD deal with me, be it ever so severely, if anything but death separates you and me." *(Ruth 1:16-17)*

Ruth, like Jonathan, did what was right in front of her with no guarantees. Ruth loved Naomi and in so doing, took her first step towards Boaz. Most would only embrace Naomi if they knew it would lead to Boaz, but that's a 'map' not a 'compass'. If you will do what's right, God will bless it even when it turns out wrong. It is always right to do the right thing even if the outcome isn't ideal.

Paul's Idea of Guidance

In Acts 16 we read about Paul leading his apostolic team on their missionary journeys: "Paul and his companions traveled all through the area of Phrygia and Galatia. The Holy Spirit had kept them from preaching the word in Asia Minor. They came to the border of Mysia. From there they tried to enter Bithynia. But the Spirit of Jesus would not let them. So they passed by Mysia. Then they went down to Troas. During the night Paul had a vision. He saw a man from Macedonia standing and begging him. "Come over to Macedonia!" the man said. "Help us!" After Paul had seen the vision, we got ready at once to leave for Macedonia. We decided that God had called us to preach the good news there." *(Acts 16:6-10)*

It seems very apparent that the great apostle Paul, who had so much revelation and to whom God revealed so many mysteries, didn't have a clue where he was going! One minute it's Asia, the next it's Bithynia. It took the entire Trinity to keep Paul out of those countries! And Paul had to be unconscious for God to eventually show him where to go.

This episode in Paul's apostolic journey proves to me that he was also a member of the second school of guidance. Paul's mentality was that everywhere was an option, everywhere was a potential 'yes' until God says 'no'. Paul simply pointed his life in the general direction of the Great Commission, 'Go into all the world'; that was his 'up'. Only when Paul was in motion did God guide him by both prevention and permission.

Please note particularly that when God prevented Paul entering Asia and Bithynia, he didn't stay there praying about why God prohibited him, he just kept moving. For Paul, trying something and it not working out was no big deal. He lived believing that his gift to God was his mobility and that God's gift to him was that he would always guide him to where he needed to be.

Guidance by Prohibition

The way God guided Paul's life in Acts 16 was what I call 'guidance by prohibition' or guidance by what God doesn't allow! This form of divine guidance is perhaps the least understood and is therefore, the most frustrating part of our lives. What God prevents, denies and keeps us away from is as much divine guidance as what he permits and opens up to us. Every door that didn't open, every opportunity you didn't get and every call that didn't come, was as much God's guidance as those that did.

When our children were small and had just started being mobile, first crawling, then walking, we guided them by prohibition. We blocked off parts of our house to prevent them from injury or danger. The stairs were forbidden, the kitchen, the fireplace and so on. Our children simply moved around in the spaces that were permitted to them, without even noticing the areas that were prohibited. This enabled us as parents to keep our children in our will without daily guidance about why that will was necessary. This, I believe, is a picture of how God for the vast majority of the time, guides our lives. Everything that is blocked, is simply to deflect us back towards what is permitted.

The only time our children ever got upset about this arrangement was when they saw one of their older siblings entering an area that was forbidden to them. I think we do this too because we don't understand that what's prohibited to us, may be permitted to someone else who is in a different place to us or who has a different mandate on their life. What's permitted to you is not intended to cause me to ask God why it's not permitted to me. God is not doing the same thing in any two lives.

Maybe you're a firm believer in the first school of guidance, but I invite you to try the second school. I can't promise that you will prefer it, but I can promise you an adventure. I can also promise that there's plenty of room in that school for millions of new Christian Entrepreneurs! Enjoy "God You Said…."

Chapter 1

THE CHRISTIAN ENTREPRENEUR & GOD'S WORD

The power source of life for the Christian Entrepreneur is the Word of God. It is the Christian Entrepreneur's responsibility to keep his or her heart with all diligence, for out of it springs the issues of life. God's Word is truly life to those that find it. He has shared His wisdom with us, and that wisdom is a tree of life to those that lay hold on it.

Many Christian Entrepreneurs lose their values of life as they climb the ladder of success. God is always interested in your success in life. But He is not interested in you losing health and family to become rich.

God's Word will motivate you to a positive and successful life. When you prosper through God's Word, you are prospering in a way that will work an eternal value in you. The wisdom of God is the Word of God. The Word of God is that tree of life that produces riches, honor, pleasantness, and peace.

There is only one way to achieve true entrepreneurial success, and that is through the Word of God. The image that God's Word builds inside the Christian Entrepreneur can become the most powerful force in your life. That image will cause you to succeed when others fail.

God You Said....
- For the word of God is living and powerful, and sharper than any two-edged sword, piercing even to the division of soul and spirit,

and of joints and marrow, and is a discerner of the thoughts and intents of the heart. *(Hebrew 4:12)*

The Christian Entrepreneur must know in his or her spirit that the word of God is first living that means it has a pulse, second it is powerful. The word "powerful" denotes something energetic, something is at work, active, and effective. It is the opposite of idle, inactive, and ineffective. Secondly, the Christian Entrepreneur must know that the word of God is sharper ***than any two-edged sword*** and in order for him or her to be successful in business depends solely on Gods word and Gods word alone.

God You Said….

- For as the rain comes down and the snow from heaven, and do not return there, but water the earth, and make it bring forth and bud, that it may give seed to the sower and bread to the eater, So shall my word be that goes forth from my mouth; it shall not return to me void, but it shall accomplish what I please, and it shall prosper in the thing for which I sent it. (*Isaiah 55:10-11*)

The Christian Entrepreneur has to understand that all increase of life within God's love comes by His Word, as human response gives place for His blessings. When the Christian Entrepreneur receives God's word, God's word of promise will never be barren or fruitless. The power in His Word will always fulfill the promise of His Word. We never need wonder how faith is developed or how fruitfulness is realized. Faith comes by "hearing" God's Word, that is, by receiving it wholeheartedly and humbly. Fruitfulness is the guaranteed by-product. God's word cannot be barren or fruitless; His own life-power is within it! The Christian Entrepreneur has to know that God's promises and plans for their businesses are as sure as being fulfilled as the fact that it rains and snows.

God You Said….

- The earth is the Lord's and all its fullness, the world and those who dwell therein. (*Psalm 24:1*)

The word fullness in the scripture refers to the earth's wealth, fertility, and inhabitants. The Christian Entrepreneur has to understand that God has dominion over all the earth, the whole creation belongs to him. This means your customers, your resources, your money, the buyers, the banks, etc. The Christian Entrepreneur simply enjoys it by God's permission. Again, the Christian Entrepreneur must know and realize that everything is owned by the Lord, and therefore fully available to His creatures for sustenance.

God You Said....

- And you shall remember the Lord your God, *for it is He who gives you power to get wealth*, that He may establish His covenant which He swore to your fore fathers, as it is this day. (*Deuteronomy 8:18*)

The word "power" means vigor, strength, force, wealth, means, or substance. Generally the word means "capacity" or "ability", whether physical, mental, or spiritual. Here Moses reminds Israel that it is God who gives to them the "ability" (power, means, endurance, capacity, wisdom) to obtain wealth, for material blessings are included in the promise to the patriarchs and their descendants, which means the Christian Entrepreneur. The Christian Entrepreneur must not falsely conclude that this capacity for success is an innate talent, but to humbly acknowledge that it is a God-given ability.

God did not promise the Christian Entrepreneur wealth, but He did promise them the power to get the wealth. Every time a thought enters your mind in regards to your business, and you act on it, that's God giving you the power to get the wealth.

God You Said....

- The heaven, even the heavens, are the Lord's; but the earth He has given to the children of men. (*Psalm 115:16*)

The Christian Entrepreneur is told in Psalm 24:1 that the earth is the Lord's and all its fullness, but Psalm 115:16 tells the Christian Entrepreneur that God gave the earth to the children of men. The Christian Entrepreneur has to understand that God is the Lord of the heavens, while men and women, are the stewards of the earth. The Christian Entrepreneur has to remember what God said in Genesis 1:26. "Let Us make man in Our image, according to Our likeness; let them have dominion over the fish of the sea, over the birds of the air, and over the cattle, over all the earth and over every creeping thing that creeps on the earth. Christian Entrepreneurs are to be God's visible representatives on the earth, ruling the business arena as God would rule it.

God You Said....

- You have made him to have dominion over the works of Your hands; You have put all things under his feet. *(Psalm 8:6)*

God has given Christian Entrepreneurs tremendous authority – to be in charge of the whole business arena. But with great authority comes great responsibility. If the Christian Entrepreneur owns a business, he or she has the legal authority to do with it as they wish, but they also have the responsibility to grow that business. How do you treat the business that God has given you? The Christian Entrepreneur must use their resources wisely because God holds them accountable for their stewardship.

God You Said....

- God is not a man, that He should lie, nor a son of man, that He should repent. Has He said, and will He not do? Or has He spoken, and will He not make it good? *(Numbers 23:19)*

The Christian Entrepreneur always has to remember that he or she is dealing with God, not a man, and God remains true to His first intention.

God You Said....

- Forever, O Lord, Your word is settled in heaven. *(Psalm 119:89)*

The Christian Entrepreneur has to know that this scripture asserts the all-encompassing, absolutely authoritative Word of God as unchangingly secured in heaven, noting: 1). The timelessness of God's rule by His Word. Though times and seasons change, though social customs, human opinions, and philosophical viewpoints vary, they have no effect on the constancy or authority of God's Word. 2). God is faithful in applying the power, promise, and blessing of His Word, along with its requirements of justice and judgment.

As the Christian Entrepreneur hears and yields to the authority of God's Word, he or she verifies that they are no longer dominated by the world's system.

God You Said....

- Your word is a lamp to my feet, and a light to my path. *(Psalm 119:105)*

The Christian Entrepreneur is inexperienced in too much of life to be without a guide. God's word is that guide. Psalm 119 unfolds manifold features of God's Word, showing how dynamically it will assist the Christian Entrepreneur in life's most practical circumstances. But no single verse focuses this more clearly than v.105, which shows how God's Word lights the way, giving the Christian Entrepreneur direction for each step ("to my feet") and giving wisdom for long-range plans ("to my path"). Let God's Word guide, correct, instruct, lead teach and confirm you. Do not hasten ahead without it.

God You Said....

- Every word of God is pure; He is a shield to those who put their trust in Him. *(Psalm 30:5)*

Here is the sufficiency of the Word of God for all the Christian Entrepreneur needs, and it is sinful to seek for spiritual light elsewhere. When men add their own fancies or their own inventions to the divine testimony, they are guilty of felony; the addition is but so much subtraction, for it perverts the meaning, it lessens the force, it modifies or destroys the original authority. The language here is similar to Ephesians 6:16, so that it may be the basis of it. Numerous times David speaks of the Lord as a shield of His saints.

God You Said....

- But He answered and said, "It is written, Man shall not live by bread alone, but by every word that proceeds from the mouth of God." *(Matthew 4:4)*

To the Christian Entrepreneur, there is a dimension to life apart from food and water, and that dimension is given life by the Word of God. God's Word provides the Christian Entrepreneur strength and the ability to grow. The Word of God adds an absolutely vital dimension to a Christian Entrepreneurs life—if he or she wants to live the abundant life and eventually have eternal life.

God You Said....

- Heaven and earth will pass away, but My words will by no means pass away. *(Matthew 24:35)*

The Christian Entrepreneur can stand on God's Word with confidence because the scriptures teach that the word of God will never pass away. This allows the Christian Entrepreneur to move freely in the marketplace. Hebrews 10:35 reminds us about our confidence, "therefore do not cast away your confidence, which has great reward."

God You Said....

- In the beginning was the Word, and the Word was with God, and the Word was God. *(John 1:1)*

The Christian Entrepreneur is reminded that in the beginning was the Word, and the Word was with God, and the Word was God and that the Word became flesh and dwelt among us and we beheld His glory (John 1:14). The Word is Jesus Christ, the eternal, ultimate expression of God. This Word allows the Christian Entrepreneur to take territory in the marketplace when aggressively acted upon.

God You Said....

- As newborn babes, desire the pure milk of the word, that you may grow thereby, if indeed you have tasted that the Lord is gracious. *(1 Peter 2:2)*

As babes hunger for milk, the Christian Entrepreneur must earnestly desire the sincere milk of the word. The spiritual milk which is without guile. This word, unadulterated, is the food upon which Christian Entrepreneurs must feed on in order to grow and sustain their businesses. So the Christian Entrepreneur must always have a thirst for God's Word and must apply it not only to their life, but also to their businesses.

God You Said....

- And they overcame him by the blood of the Lamb and by the word of their testimony, and they did not love their lives to the death. *(Revelation 12:11)*

The Christian Entrepreneur will overcome the devil by appropriating the victory of the finished work of Christ, and by the public confession of their faith and patient endurance, even in the face of trials in the marketplace. The Christian Entrepreneurs constant posture under the authority of the Cross's victory by the blood of the Lamb and steadfastness to the promise and authority of God's Word (the word of your testimony) is the key to their overcoming. The presence of the Kingdom at this time calls each Christian Entrepreneur to responsible spiritual warfare and anticipated victories.

God You Said....

- Beloved, I pray that you may prosper in all things and be in health, just as your soul prospers. *(3 John 2)*

It is very clear that God wants the Christian Entrepreneur to prosper. However, prosperity should not be the end in itself. It ought to be the result of a quality of life, commitment, dedication, and action that is in line with God's word. In this text the word "prosper" literally means "to help on the road" or "succeed in reaching." It clearly implies that divine prosperity is not a momentary, passing phenomenon, *but rather it is an ongoing, progressing state of success and well-being*. It is intended for every area of our lives; the spiritual, the physical, the emotional, and the material. However, God does not want the Christian Entrepreneur to unduly emphasize any one area. He or she must maintain a balance.

God You Said....

- For the eyes of the Lord run to and fro throughout the whole earth, to show Himself strong on behalf of those whose heart is loyal to Him. *(2 Chronicles 16:9)*

The Lord diligently searches for Christian Entrepreneurs whom He can bless because they have shown themselves loyal to His call.

God You Said....

- My brethren, count it all joy when you fall into various trials, knowing that the testing of your faith produces patience. But let patience have its perfect work, that you may be perfect and complete, lacking nothing. If any of you lacks wisdom, let him ask of God, who gives to all liberally and without reproach, and it will be given to him. But let him ask in faith, with no doubting, for he who doubts is like a wave of the sea driven and tossed by the wind. For let not that man suppose that he will receive anything from the Lord; he is a double-minded man, unstable in all his ways. *(James 1:2-8)*

As with anything else, being a Christian Entrepreneur does not automatically exclude you from difficulties. The proper attitude in meeting adversity in your business is to count it all joy, which is not an emotional reaction, but a deliberate intelligent appraisal of the situation from God's perspective, viewing trials or set backs in your business as a means of moral and spiritual growth. We do not rejoice in the trials themselves, but in their possible results (growth in your business, full staff of workers, multiple locations, etc.).

The Christian Entrepreneur has to understand that testing carries the idea of proving genuineness and that trials serve as a discipline to purge faith of dross, stripping away anything that is false.

Patience is not a passive resignation to adverse circumstances, but a positive steadfastness that bravely endures.

A double-minded man is a person drawn in two opposite directions. His allegiance is divided and because of his lack of sincerity he vacillates between belief and disbelief, sometimes thinking that God will help him, and at other times giving up all hope in Him. The Christian Entrepreneur has to remain steady and believe that He who has begun a good work in you is faithful to complete it until the day of Jesus Christ. God did not have you to start a business to fail.

God You Said....

- The steps of a good man are ordered by the Lord, And He delights in his way. Though he fall, he shall not be utterly cast down; For the Lord upholds him with His hand. (*Psalm 37:23-24*)

The Christian Entrepreneur in whom God delights is one who follows God, trusts Him, and tries to do His will. God watches over and makes firm every step that person takes. If the Christian Entrepreneur would like to have God direct their way, then they have to seek His advice before they step out.

God You Said....

- The grass withers, the flower fades, but the word of our God stands forever. (*Isaiah 40:8*)

These words *"but the word of our God stands forever"* offer full assurance of the reliability, stability, and the eternal nature of the divine word. God's word is eternal and unfailing, the world system changes and is unreliable, but God's Word is constant. It's only in God's eternal Word will we, the Christian Entrepreneur, find lasting solutions to our problems and needs. The Christian Entrepreneur has to know that the word of God has the final authority. If God calls your business successful, then your business is successful. If God calls you the head and not the tale, then you and your business are the head and not the tale.

God You Said....

- For I am the Lord, I do not change. (*Malachi 3:6*)

The Christian Entrepreneur has to know that God is immutable, which means unchanging and unchangeable. His purposes do not change. He never grows in knowledge or wisdom. He never differs from Himself. He never improves upon His own perfection. God is always wise, always sovereign, always good, always just, always holy, always merciful, and always gracious. Whatever God is, He always is. There are no "sometimes" attributes of God. All of His attributes are "always" attributes. He always is what He is. He never makes excuses. He never has to because He always keeps His promises. The Christian Entrepreneur may rely upon God to keep His word!

God You Said….

- So then each of us shall give account of himself to God. *(Romans 14:12)*

The Christian Entrepreneur must "give account of himself". That is, of his character and conduct; his words and actions; his plans and purposes. Every work and purpose shall be brought forth, and tried by the unerring standard of justice. Did you stand on God's word to grow your business? Did you treat God's people godly? Did you get up and try again?

God You Said….

- And those who know Your name will put their trust in You; For You, Lord, have not forsaken those who seek You. *(Psalm 9:10)*

The safest and strongest protection that the Christian Entrepreneur has is the name of the Lord. The Christian Entrepreneur has to remember that God forsook His Son for them. Jesus said from the cross, "My God, My God, why have You forsaken Me?" (Matthew 27:46). Has it ever occurred to you that the only person God ever really forsook was His own Son? He who did not spare His own Son, but delivered Him up for us all" (Romans 8:32). Because He did this, we can, the Christian Entrepreneur, be sure He will never forsake us for the sake of His Son. The safest place in all the world is in the will of God, and the safest protection in all the world is the name of God. Your business is designed for greatness.

God You Said....
- Before I formed you in the womb I knew you; before you were born I sanctified you. (*Jeremiah 1:5*)

The Christian Entrepreneur has been set apart according to God's predestination and hidden purpose; that is, they are by special counsel, designed for their work, and what they are designed for, they are fitted for. God destines them to it, and forms them for it, when He first formed the spirit of man within him. God chose the Christian Entrepreneur to be a successful business person and run a successful business. Just like Jeremiah, the Christian Entrepreneur has been called from above, but let him know that he who gave him his commission is the same that gave him his being, that *formed him in the belly* and brought him *forth out of the womb*, that therefore He was his rightful owner and might employ him and make use of him as He pleased, and that this commission was given him in pursuance of the purpose God had purposed in Himself concerning him. The great Creator knows what use to make of every man before He makes him. He has made all for Himself, and of the same lumps of clay designs a vessel of honor or dishonor, as He pleases. What God has designed men for He will call them to; for His purposes cannot be frustrated. Known unto God are all His own works beforehand, and His knowledge is infallible and His purpose unchangeable. The Christian Entrepreneur has been appointed for a particular work, "I formed thee not only a man, but a successful businessman."

God You Said....
- Now to Him who is able to do exceedingly abundantly above all that we ask or think, according to the power that works in us. (*Ephesians 3:20*)

The Apostle Paul prayed for believers to know that order of reformation or revival that brings about an intensification of the presence and power of Jesus Christ. In this text, Paul asked that the Holy Spirit deepen His work in our lives in three ways: 1). That Christ would dwell – more literally, "be at home" in our hearts by faith, that is, that He would move from being an acquaintance to being the center of the Christian Entrepreneurs life; 2). That we would grasp God's love at a spiritual level, beyond intellectual or theological knowledge; and 3). That we would be filled with God's fullness, that is, that the Holy Spirit would reveal the things of Christ more fully, achieving God's fuller work in each life – unhindered, unquenched, and ungrieved.

God You Said....
• The race is not to the swift, nor the battle to the strong, nor bread to the wise, nor riches to men of understanding, nor favor to men of skill; but time and chance happen to them all. *(Ecclesiastes 9:11)*

The fastest runner doesn't always win the race, and the strongest warrior doesn't always win the battle. The wise sometimes go hungry, and the skillful are not necessarily wealthy. And those who are educated don't always lead successful lives. It is all decided by chance, by being in the right place at the right time. Time and chance happen to them all. A sovereign Providence breaks men's measures, and blasts their hopes, and teaches them that the way of man is not in himself, but subject to the divine will. We must use means, but not trust in them; if we succeed, we must give God the praise (Psalm 44:3); if we be crossed, we must acquiesce in His will and take our lot.

God You Said....
• For of Him and through Him and to Him are all things, to whom be glory forever, Amen. *(Romans 11:36)*

All things, the universe, ourselves, our businesses, our salvation, and everything else, all are from God and work through His sustaining power, and ultimately further His glory. The proper response of every creature and even the Christian Entrepreneur is to give God glory forever.

God You Said....
• For the gifts and the calling of God are irrevocable. *(Romans 11:29)*

The Christian Entrepreneur is anointed to make money, anointed to dominate the marketplace, anointed to change the commonwealth of the world and they are anointed and equipped to change lives. God says that the gifts and calling are irrevocable. He will not take them back. Go and take what God has given you.

God You Said....

- For as a man thinks in his heart, so is he. *(Proverbs 23:7)*

The heart, being the motive center of the whole man, determines what he really is. Outward appearances mean little, for hypocrisy is easy to every person, but what he thinks in his heart when no one but God can see, reveals his real character. The Christian Entrepreneur must think like God and act like God. This is only achieved through hearing God's Word, reading God's Words, studying God's Word, memorizing God's Word and mediating on God's Word.

God You Said....

- Where there is no vision, the people perish. *(Proverbs 29:18)*

When the Christian Entrepreneur lacks any revelation from God (divine insight), he or she is destined to struggle in the things of God for his or her business.

God You Said....

- Death and life are in the power of the tongue, and those who love it will eat its fruit. *(Proverbs 18:21)*

The Christian Entrepreneurs life largely reflects the fruit of his or her tongue. To speak life is to speak God's perspective on any issue of your business; to speak death is to declare life's negatives, to declare defeat, or complain constantly over your business.

God You Said....

- And do not be conformed to this world, but be transformed by the renewing of your mind, that you may prove what is that good and acceptable and perfect will of God. *(Romans 12:2)*

A. *The Christian Entrepreneur is changed morally (12:2)*

"Be not conformed to this world," says Paul. The word "conformed" refers to the act of an individual assuming an outward expression that does not come from within him, nor is it representative of his inner heart life. It lays stress on that which is external. We are not to be fashioned by the world. The Christian Entrepreneur cannot let the world around them squeeze them into its own mold. The word for "world" here "signifies the condition of humanity, which, since the fall, is in spiritual darkness, with a nature, tendencies, and influences controlled by the powers of darkness in opposition to God, and now under the prince of this world. The world is the devil's lair for sinners and his lure for saints.

The Christian Entrepreneur whose body has been laid on the altar of God will not be conformed to the world. They are morally changed. Their life is not molded from without but from within. Jesus provided us with a picturesque illustration when speaking of Solomon, He pointed to the flowers of the field and said, "Solomon in all his glory was not arrayed like one of these" (Matthew 6:29). Solomon's splendor was put on from without; the glory of the lily grows from within. The Christian Entrepreneur has an inward power to overcome the pressures of the world, and their presented body makes it possible for that power to be unleashed. They are not molded by the world's morals; they set the standards for the world.

B. *The Christian Entrepreneur is changed mentally (12:2)*

"Be ye transformed by the renewing of your mind," says Paul. This is a call for a transfigured life. The Greek word translated in "transformed" in this passage occurs in only three other places in the New Testament. It is used to describe the transfiguration of the Lord Jesus (Matthew 17:2; Mark 9:2) and it is used to describe the glorious change wrought in the Christian Entrepreneur when he or she steadfastly contemplates the Lord Jesus (2 Corinthians 3:18).

There has to be a metamorphosis, metamorphosis means a "change of form or change of character." An example is the caterpillar which undergoes metamorphosis in its chrysalis and emerges a glorious butterfly. The same creature which enters the filmy tomb eventually emerges, but the change is so remarkable that it cannot be recognized as the same. It is this kind of change the Holy Spirit wishes to work in the life of the Christian Entrepreneur, but to do it He must have control of the body and free access to the mind.

C. The Christian Entrepreneur is changed motivationally (12:2)

"That ye may prove what is that good, and acceptable and perfect will of God." Every Christian Entrepreneur is responsible to discover for him or herself the will of God for their life. Through the process of their daily communion with the Lord they discover some aspect of the revealed will of God, they will embrace it, because it is good. God cannot ask us to do anything that is not for our eternal good. The demand may cut right across our opinions, our ambitions, and our tastes.

It is also acceptable. God will not ask us to do that which we cannot accept. In Abraham we find an example of how acceptable God's will is, God asking him to offer up Isaac as a burnt offering. Hard as the demand was, Abraham considered the will of God to be acceptable. He did not know why God demanded this sacrifice, nor did he know how God would make good His promises which were all centered in Isaac. But he did believe that God could raise Isaac from the dead (Hebrews 11:17-19) even though he had no actual guarantee that he would. He accepted God's will without question.

Finally, God's will is perfect. No plan of ours can improve on the plan of God. We only see bits and pieces; He sees the whole. We see only fragments of the past. We measure things by the narrow horizon of our present vision. He sees past, present and future in its total context as related to eternity. He sees when, where and why we touch the lives of others. He weighs all actions. He controls all circumstances.

So then, the Christian Entrepreneur is both challenged and changed as a believer. He or she presents their body to God and takes on a whole new, higher, greater dimension of living. How this new quality of life touches the marketplace is yet to be revealed.

God You Said....

- Your words are what sustain me. They bring me great joy and are my heart's delight, for I bear your name, O Lord God Almighty. *(Jeremiah 15:16)*

The Christian Entrepreneur and his or her business, will only be sustained by God's word. Here Jeremiah received God's word as food; he cheerfully received them, treasured them up in his memory, digested them in his mind, and carefully retained them. The word of God is food to the Christian Entrepreneurs soul. The word of God is sweet, savory, wholesome, nourishing, and strengthening; not as merely heard externally, or only assented unto, or superficially tasted of; but when eaten, will produce much fruit for the Christian Entrepreneur. The Word, unless it is mixed with faith is not profitable.

<u>Things To Remember</u>

God's Word Is A Seed

Most people expect God's Word to work like a stick of dynamite -- but God's Word is like a seed. We know because of what Jesus said in Luke 8:11, "Now the parable is this: The seed is the word of God.

The Holy Spirit, through Peter, also said God's Word is a seed in I Peter 1:23, "having been born again, not of corruptible seed but incorruptible, through the word of God which lives and abides forever"

God's Word is alive. Just like a seed -- the Bible is full of unseen life. John 6:63 "It is the Spirit who gives life; the flesh profits nothing. The words that I speak to you are spirit, and they are life.

Jesus said His words are alive. They contain life. The words in your Bible may look lifeless and powerless. Seeds do, too. But they are not without life or power.

In Mark 4:30-31, Jesus explained that the Kingdom of God works like a seed. So, if we are to understand God's Kingdom and how He operates, we need to understand seeds.

Seeds

A seed is alive: it contains life. Your physical senses are incapable of judging whether a seed is alive or not. You cannot see, feel, hear, smell, or taste the life in a seed. There is only one way to prove a seed is alive -- plant it.

A seed does nothing until planted. Seeds do not grow sitting in a sack on your shelf. They must be planted in the proper place. If you desire the Word of God to produce in your life, *you* must decide to plant the Word in your heart and mind.

The best way for the Christian Entrepreneur to plant the seed of God's Word in their life is by speaking the Word. Hearing others speak the Word is good -- but this will not produce as bountiful a harvest as you speaking the Word yourself.

Speaking God's Word with your mouth is essential. As we speak God's Word we are planting the seed in our heart for the harvest of results we desire. Romans 10:10 "For with the heart one believes to righteousness, and with the mouth confession is made to salvation."

A seed is much smaller than the plant it produces. The problem you face may seem huge. In comparison, a scripture may seem very small. But when planted, that Word will grow in you and overcome the problem.

A seed always produces after its kind. Galatians 6:7 "Do not be deceived, God is not mocked; for whatever a man sows, that he will also reap."

Whatever you need, or desire, find scriptures relating to that. Then plant those scriptures inside you in abundance. Those seeds will grow up and produce a harvest of what you need or desire.

A seed is powerful. As a seed begins to grow, it will push up dirt, rocks, etc. Whatever the obstacles are, God's Word planted in your heart will push them out of the way.

A seed begins its growth in secret (underground). The only way to tell if a seed is growing is to dig it up, or wait for a plant to appear. If you dig up a seed, you may kill it.

A seed takes time to produce. No one expects a seed to produce a harvest the same day that seed is planted. Sometimes the Word of God seems to spring up and bear fruit immediately. Yet, if we knew the details, we would understand that the fruit of the Word grew in that person's life over time.

A seed is persistent. A seed never gives up, but works day and night. Even when you are sleeping, the seed you have planted is working to grow and express itself in a fruitful harvest.

A seed is not affected by other seeds. Whatever happens to other seeds does not make any difference to a specific seed. Each seed sticks to its own task. One wheat seed planted in a corn field will still produce wheat. Seed do not become discouraged, or quit, even if other seeds die.

A seed will stop growing without nourishment. Planting a seed is not enough to assure a harvest. Seeds must be protected and taken care of until harvest time. A seed which is dug up, or not watered, will not produce.

More seeds planted produce a larger harvest. 2 Corinthians 9:6 "But this I say: He who sows sparingly will also reap sparingly, and he who sows bountifully will also reap bountifully."

Chapter 2

THE CHRISTIAN ENTREPRENEUR & PRAYER

What is Prayer and why do we pray? Prayer is focused energy. Developing a healthy prayer life is part of the dedication that is required for the journey on the spiritual path to entrepreneurial success. Prayer can take many forms-formal, informal, casual, elegant, spoken, silent. All are acceptable, and all are heard. There is no right way for the Christian Entrepreneur to pray. However, some prayers can be extremely powerful. If it comes from the heart, and you understand the laws of energy, prayer can be truly miraculous for the Christian Entrepreneur.

Prayer is a powerful energy. It not only connects the Christian Entrepreneur to the force greater than self, but it stimulates the power of creative energy within the Entrepreneur and puts into action his or her ability to create. You literally merge energies with the Creator. You step beyond limitations and into the realm of possibilities. It is a powerful means of adding energy to one's desires. Thought forms emerge and energy multiplies. The more faith and trust the Christian Entrepreneur has, the faster thoughts manifest into physical reality.

Prayer literally takes you out of your body and the linear mind controlling it, into the nonlinear space of the Spirit. It allows you to open up and to expect that things can be created that do not yet exist, even things beyond your current grasp of understanding. Your soul knows this. Prayer serves as a passageway out of the concrete mind and into the realm of possibilities.

The act of prayer is an expression of your confidence in a larger divine order and in the significance of your own existence. It expresses a faith in life and life's experiences. As you walk the spiritual path, you develop a respect for a force greater than self. You learn to love life in all of its forms and to treat life with respect and reverence. Prayer becomes an overt way to express this growing awareness to yourself and to the universe.

The longing of the soul for connection is answered in prayer. It is the foundation for spiritual connection. If you desire connection, prayer must be built into your life in a way that will withstand the daily pressures and interruptions of life. The quantity of time is not important; the priority is.

God You Said....

- But you, when you pray, go into your room, and when you have shut your door, pray to your Father who is in the secret place; and your Father who sees in secret will reward you openly. *(Matthew 6:6)*

In the NT, Jesus presents devotion as a matter of the heart. He contrasts sincere, heartfelt devotion with the external, hypocritical, pretentious practices of piety among the Pharisees. He warns His disciples against allowing even genuine, good works to distract them from wholehearted devotion to Him. The Christian Entrepreneur must understand that devotion is a matter of developing an intimate relationship with the living God.

The Christian Entrepreneur has to experience times of private prayer. A private place for personal prayer and devotions are times for communion with God. The Entrepreneurs business will not advance without it. In Matthew 26:40-41, Jesus said to Peter in the Garden of Gethsemane "What? Could you not watch with Me one hour?" "Watch and pray, lest you enter into temptation, The spirit indeed is willing, but the flesh is weak." Everything the Christian Entrepreneur needs is in the Secret Place and once you leave that Secret Place expect God to move on your behalf in your business (new customers, new territories, more employees, more resources, more sales, etc).

God You Said....
- And whatever things you ask in prayer, believing, you will receive. *(Matthew 21:22)*

The "mountainous" obstacles or opposition that Christian Entrepreneurs are destined to face as leaders would call for active and secure "faith in God" (Mark 11:22). Here Jesus is teaching His disciples that faith works miracles and is the basis for answered prayer.

God You Said....
- Ask, and it will be given to you; seek, and you will find; knock, and it will be opened to you. For everyone who asks receives, and he who seeks finds, and to him who knocks it will be opened. *(Matthew 7:7-8)*

The Greek imperatives, ask, seek, and knock are in the present tense, suggesting continued petition. Jesus tells us to persist in pursuing God. Christian Entrepreneurs often give up after a few halfhearted efforts and conclude that God cannot be found. But knowing God takes faith, focus, and follow-though, and Jesus assures us that we will be rewarded. The Christian Entrepreneur should not give up on their efforts to seek God, continue to ask Him for more knowledge, patience, direction, creativity, ideas, and resources and He will give them to you.

God You Said....
- Blessed is the man who listens to me, watching daily at my gates, waiting at the posts of my doors. For whoever finds me finds life, and obtains favor from the Lord. *(Proverbs 8:34-35)*

The Christian Entrepreneur who discovers wisdom has found a priceless treasure. Wisdom offers blessing and life to those who heed her, but cursing and death to those who hate her. Wisdom's gracious invitation is more desirable than anything and is a invitation to a blessed life.

God You Said....
- I love those who love me, and those who seek me diligently will find me. *(Proverbs 8:17)*

The Christian Entrepreneur should seek God early with sincere affection and diligence, which He mentions as the evidence of their love. We are to study the word of God diligently, and with a desire to profit. Seek Him early, seek Him earnestly, seek Him before any thing else. Those who love Christ, are such as have seen His loveliness, and have had His love shed abroad in their hearts; therefore they are happy. They shall be happy in this world, or in that which is beyond.

God You Said....

- But know that the Lord has set apart for Himself him who is godly; the Lord will hear when I call to Him. *(Psalm 4:3)*

The godly, the Christian Entrepreneur is precious, therefore they are set apart for God. Know that the Lord hath set apart him that is godly for Himself. We set apart things that are precious; the godly, the Christian Entrepreneur is set apart as God's peculiar treasure. The Lord will hear them when they cry out to Him.

God You Said....

- Evening, and morning, and at noon, will I pray, and cry aloud: and He shall hear my voice. *(Psalm 55:17)*

The Hebrew day started at evening, so this list is in the correct order for the Christian Entrepreneur to pray all day long. Although the Christian Entrepreneur is not tied down to these exact and precise times of prayer, yet this teaches us that we ought to pray frequently and constantly, and that a day should not pass without it; and the morning and evening seem to be very proper seasons for it, seeing the mercies of the Lord are new every morning; and we should be thankful for them and the mercies of the night past, and implore divine protection and grace for the day following; and at evening we should express our thankfulness for the mercies of the day, and commit ourselves and families into the hands of God, who is the Christian Entrepreneurs Keeper, that neither slumbers nor sleeps.

This book will be an important resource for those with a life-threatening condition and for the people that care for them. Dr. Penny's love and compassion is reflected through every word written in *"Healing Hope for Grief and Bereavement"* and I admire how she has given from the depth of her heart and tried her best to bring comfort and hope in such a time as in death and dying. *I highly recommend this creative work* toall who face the challenges of personal grief or providing quality care at life's final moments to loved ones or in their professions.

Gregory C. Townsend
Former Administrator, Birmingham Area Hospice

Dr. Penny Njoroge, who I lovingly refer to as Dr. Penny, has written an astounding masterpiece that teaches individuals how to use spirituality to cope with grief. Dr. Penny's thoughtful insight and sensitivity is exhibited throughout this work. Anyone facing a grieving situation would do well to read this guiding manual. This classic is a must read for all humans because we will face a grieving period at some time in our lifetime as a result of a death of a loved one or for many other diverse challenges . Congratulations Dr. Penny on a job well done. *You have definitely made grieving a little easier to cope with!!!!!!*

Dr. Charles Fields
President, Fields & Associates, Inc.

Dr. Penny Njoroge has been a leader among leaders in the American Pain Foundation Network for several years. As the State Leader for Alabama, Dr. Penny is part of a national grassroots advocacy effort working to raise awareness about the hidden epidemic of the under-treatment of pain and promoting positive pain policy and practice. She works tirelessly to shed light on the darkness of damaging misconceptions, speaks passionately for those who are without a voice and skillfully works with others to remove barriers to appropriate pain care. In her book *"Healing Hope For Your Grief and Bereavement"*, she brings her wealth of experience, compassion and passion that will inspire readers to embrace grief and healing with the same ways she has been a beacon of inspiration for others working to improve pain care. We applaud the inclusion of a chapter on pain care as it provides valuable information and powerful stories from a truly cross-cultural perspective. Out of her own personal experience with chronic pain, Dr. Penny passionately highlights and voices the deep impact of grief that chronic pain brings to millions who suffer silently in hiding for fear of being ridiculed and seen as weaklings when they acknowledge it and seek help. Her words give a vivid picture of the tragic impact of the lack of pain care has for individuals, families, friends and communities. As is true throughout her book, Dr. Penny weaves messages of hope and inspiration for all of us to urgently transform our compassion into action to improve the lives of others. *This is definitely a book worth reading and recommending to family and friends.*

Mary Bennett, MFA
Director of Grassroots Advocacy
American Pain Foundation

As a Registered Nurse, I often encounter the terminally ill, the dying and grieving families in my work. Reading through this book has both challenged and helped me. Not only is the title capturing but the book contents are very enticing for everyone both as a professional helping others through such experiences or for those personally undergoing grief for one reason or another. Dr. Penny is not only humble and visionary, but is also encouraging, intelligent, uplifting and very articulate in her writing. She effectively teaches in her book what and when to say in such circumstances and comes out as a very compassionate and caring person to everyone reading this book. Dr. Penny has been honored numerous times and received many distinguished awards including a **Head of State Commendation (HSC)** from the President of The Republic of Kenya for her work in the community, in her counseling the grieving, the broken hearted and those challenged by all kinds of problems. In a very soft spoken approach, she has comforted and reassured numerous people undergoing life shattering experiences and is well known in the community for reaching out to others in crisis situations. She is also very effective and passionate in empowering and motivating people in helpless\hopeless circumstances to rise up from the ashes of their pain and learn to live beyond their tragedies. **THIS BOOK IS A MUST READ for everyone.**

Mary Mathangani, RN, CN
Trinity Hospital, Birmingham, Al

To know Dr. Penny Njoroge means having a kindred relationship with someone who speaks directly from the heart. She expresses genuine concern for others, meets everyone with a smile and greets you with warmth and acceptance. She has a deeply nurturing spirit and her words are sincere and encouraging. She is good at empowering others to survive painful situations to become living testimonies of God's healing hope and grace.

Dr. Penny embodies a spirit of giving back and reaching out to those in need. Although her life requires her to comfort those who are bereaved, she is talented and naturally gifted in her ministry of HOPE as she exemplifies a mission to aid, support and nurture those in pain and struggle.

She is well aware of the ingredients essential to overcome grief by the continuous counsel and ministry from the word of God. This book, *Healing Hope for Your Grief & Bereavement,* is a true and down to earth testament of her daily work and walk through life. Dr. Penny is constantly working in the vineyard of the Lord by helping others to overcome that which we must all face at one point or another as we journey through life.

Dr. Penny is well informed and knowledgeable on the matters of grief and bereavement from her professional, practical and daily walk with the terminally ill, the dying and those left behind to mourn and grieve their loved ones. She is very caring, compassionate and tender with others at such moments. Dr. Penny has left lasting impressions on many people's lives through her ministry wherever she has worked, and is highly respected by everyone both at work and in our community at large. She has received a lot of honors and recognition for her highly effective ministry. *I HIGHLY RECOMMEND THIS BOOK TO EVERYONE.*

Sandra Owens
Risk Management Coordinator
St. Vincent's East Hospital

HEALING HOPE
FOR YOUR GRIEF
& BEREAVEMENT

Dr. Penny Wanjiru Njoroge

WestBow
PRESS
A DIVISION OF THOMAS NELSON

WestBow Press books may be ordered through booksellers or by contacting:

WestBow Press
A Division of Thomas Nelson
1663 Liberty Drive
Bloomington, IN 47403
www.westbowpress.com
1-(866) 928-1240

Because of the dynamic nature of the Internet, any Web addresses or links contained in this book may have changed since publication and may no longer be valid. The views expressed in this work are solely those of the author and do not necessarily reflect the views of the publisher, and the publisher hereby disclaims any responsibility for them.

ISBN: 978-1-4497-0450-6 (sc)
ISBN: 978-1-4497-0621-0 (e)

Library of Congress Control Number: 2010935751

Printed in the United States of America

WestBow Press rev. date: 9/10/2010

I would like to dedicate this book to a few people who God specifically put in my life for a very divine and humbling purpose for my spiritual life and walk.

I am for ever grateful for my father Lawrence and mother Miriam who have both left this life and taken their eternal resting places in heaven. It was my parents who constantly reminded me throughout their presence in my life that "Quitting was not an option" and despite the adversities I will face in my journey, God's divine plans and destiny for my life would never change or fail, if I remained focused and connected with Him. It is their loving soft voices of encouragement that have kept me going when I felt like quitting as the Master Potter melted and molded me into the person I am today. I will always honor their names and thank God for their permanent prints on my life.

The best and priceless gifts in my life are my six children, each of who is a unique and precious jewel. Paul, Lawrence, Stella, Evelyn, Eric and Mary have all stood faithfully and in steadfast love and care during the most trying seasons as I traveled through my personal valleys of both grief and bereavement. Each of them fully aware of, not only my strengths but my worst weaknesses, have given me devoted love and support as I faced my giants in tears and frustrations and constantly reminded me that with God's promised help, I had the capacity to make it in life. They stood by me at the worst moment of my life as I battled a painful divorce after 30 years of marriage. At my most vulnerable moments when all I prayed for was to die, they stuck it out with me and gave me no other choice but to survive and celebrate their children, my grandchildren. I am humbled and grateful because were it not for them, I would never have lived long enough to see the greatest miracles in my life. I owe the completion of this book to them because they have been the best cheerleaders I would have prayed for in moments when I wanted to shelve the manuscript and forget all about it. I passionately dedicate this book to each of them.

Finally, I dedicate this book to my most beautiful grandchildren Ayanna, Shayna, Ava, Jonathan and the precious one who should be joining our family in a couple of months. The birth of each of them has heralded a new beginning for me and a renewed meaning for life. They are each a silver lining in my challenging moments and for them I bless God for my future generations. I dedicate this book to them and those who come into my life hereafter. For all the above and my many friends, I thank God for their undying support.

CONTENTS

FOREWORD

First and foremost, I give thanks to God our almighty Father for His goodness and love. He has been my provider and my protector. I would not be where I am today, if I had not been strong in my faith. God's covering has helped me to weather the *storm*! It would have been a blessing to me and made some of my own struggles easier to deal with if I had Dr. Penny's words to guide me, as well as, my family. Her book, *Healing Hope for Grief and Bereavement*, provides encouraging words and details examples of how to first acknowledge what is or has happened to you and how best to deal with it. I have read it and it is powerful and encouraging!

I am 45 years old and have experienced loss at various levels: both parents, grandparents, best friends, and a sister-in-law. The most difficult for me was growing up without my parents. Both of my parents died a tragic death at such a young age. I am the oldest of four children and was just shy of 5 years old when they died. I remember going to their funerals, the burial, and even asking my grandmother where my mom was and when she was coming back home. I recall her vividly saying," your mom is in heaven." At such a young age, I really did not understand why she was not coming home. There were many nights I cried for my mom and dad. I just could not understand why they were gone and why my cousins and friends had their parents and I did not.

My grandparents were God fearing people and did a great job taking care of me and my three siblings. As I look back, if I had to choose three things that helped me heal over the years, I would say it was God, being able to forgive, and my grandparent's open and honest conversations about my parents and life in general. Dr. Penny also talks about open and honest conversations in her book. Having the strength to talk about what hurts you the most is part of the healing process. The worst thing that you can do is not acknowledge that you are grieving and not be willing to talk about how you feel. I think of my parents everyday and often find myself starring at the family photo taken the Christmas before their death. I often wonder how and if my life would have been different if they had lived. Life has been great and I have been blessed with a wonderful family, very close friends, and a very successful career. I married my high school sweetheart and have two beautiful children. In the midst of it all, every child and adult longs for their mother and father. I still do, but in a healthy and spiritual way.

I have experienced many other facets of loss and grief that are too many to detail. If you are reading the foreword of this book, you have taken the first step in acknowledging that either you personally or someone you know needs spiritually guided steps to grief recovery and bereavement. I wish you much success and stress that you keep the Word of God in your heart and allow Him to guide your steps.

Peace and Blessings,

Dr. Carol Jefferson Ratcliffe, RN, CNOR, FACHE

INTRODUCTION

Life itself is mystifying, but one thing that is certain is that we all will experience loss. When this occurs, it takes on a new meaning for each of us. ***Healing Hope for Grief and Bereavement*** takes us through life's journey that we all will face or have the potential to face at some point in our lives. It requires faith, hope, support, and inner strength to overcome and deal with death, separation, or even divorce. What may be a simple adjustment for one person may take a lifetime of transition for another. You simply need to understand that this is o.k. Men and women, children, teenagers, and people with different ethnic backgrounds respond differently in their adaptation to loss and grief and how they heal.

Through ***Healing Hope for Grief and Bereavement.*** Dr. Penny gives real life examples, transcending through the stages and processes of grief and types of loss, with guidance on how to heal the hurt and pain and your soul. Self preservation is an important component to your success along the continuum of healing. Through life and this book, Dr. Penny also helps you to learn that it is acceptable to cry, to talk about how you feel, and to seek the help of a medical professional. The Word of God resonates throughout this book as a constant reminder that you are never alone. Seek His help and you shall find solace in His Word. Life is full of challenges and many are difficult to overcome. When you take the initial step to help yourself or allow someone else to help you, you are well on your way! Remember, that God loves you and He will grant you a new beginning.

The book is well written with many illustrations from different aspects of life and I would recommend it for everyone. If you have not yet experienced grief and loss it will give you some ideas on how to be an effective support for others in their moments of grief and bereavement. I also prepares you for that inevitable day or season when we must each travel through that valley of grief, pain and tribulation for one reason or another. Dr. Penny also helps you understand why people respond the way they do in their different moments of struggle and brokenness.

1

THE IMPACT OF DEATH, DYING, & GRIEF

As I sit and reflect on this topic, it quietly dawns on me that whoever walks through life must inevitably experience a moment of grief for one reason or another. And this goes for all the living creatures of the earth. From the huge elephants to the minute insects like the ants etc. In the African jungles, the huge elephants have been known to linger around a dead mate, offspring or parent for days, refusing to move, overcome with grief, loss and sadness, until the shock subsides and a sense of acceptance takes over.

Children and adults alike, have been know to grieve the loss of a beloved pet so painfully as if a fellow human being had passed away. Wherever there has been some form of relationship and friendship; separation by death, divorce or other will inevitably cause pain, grief and trauma especially if not adequately dealt with.

The pain of loosing to death a parent, a child, a spouse/partner, a sibling or close friend, colleague or neighbor has a tendency of shaking up the very roots of our lives, turbulently.

The extent of the grief will depend on the relationship that existed with the deceased.

In many cultures, death is not an easy topic of discussion. Across the universe, people avoid talking about death almost as if you can avoid it by not talking or thinking about it. Or as if when you talk about it you call or draw it upon yourself or those that we love. The reality is that either way, every human being has a destiny with death.

The bible tells us that there is a time and a place for everything in life. A time to be born and a time to die. Under the same token, a time to celebrate the birth of a new baby into our lives and families but inevitably for this same baby there will be a time to mourn or grieve for their departure out of our lives and back to their creator God. I say this as a believer, knowing that through the death of Jesus Christ on the cross, God made a provision for us to go back home for which we were all made. Yes, into an endless and timeless eternity with him, never to grieve, loose our loved ones again. Never to feel the brokenness, helplessness, hopelessness etc that accompany us through grief and bereavement. In the meantime, the Lord promises to heal the broken hearted and bind their wounds (Psalm 147:3). Like David in his many crossroads of grief and heartache despite being "A man after God's own Heart", we need to ask God "May your gracious spirit lead me forward on a firm footing" as I travel through this grief (Psalm 143:10b)"

The flesh and blood in us will mourn and grieve but will also be sustained by the hope of seeing our beloved departed brothers in their new and glorified forms when I too join them after my death, to be mourned by those I leave behind.

Grief is therefore an unavoidable circle into which we must some day enter. I have lost many friends in life, but the death of my two younger brothers 14 and three years ago followed by both of my parents one after the other within 4 months gave death, dying and grief a very personal meaning. It has touched my life directly and personally. My work as a hospice/hospital chaplain has also exposed me to this monster as a minister, counselor and pastoral support on a full time basis. The truth is that one can never get used or comfortable with death, no matter how often you see or experience it daily. The finality and separation through death is an experience like no other.

As we deal with any and all kinds of losses, God may feel so far away. We might even wonder in our brokenness if God really understands or cares about our sorrow. And if so, we wonder why we have to part with all those we love. But in Isaiah 53:3-6 we read that He (Jesus) was a man of sorrows, rejected and despised, acquainted with bitterest grief. He has borne our grief and carried our sorrow. By His stripes we are healed.

Dealing with grief is almost like going through deep and turbulent waters that threaten to swallow you. It may also feel like going through intensely hot fires that are almost consuming you. Yet in Isaiah 43:1-5 God promises his protection and covering for our safety. While we may never forget or fully recover from our losses, grief or bereavement, things will gradually get better and bearable as time goes by. But how and at what pace this happens is unique to every person. There is therefore no A-Z method of grief and recovery set on hard stone. We must allow ourselves to process our grief in our own individual ways.

2

EXPERIENCING THE DEATH OF A LOVED ONE

There are many taboo subjects in many cultures across the universe, but death is yet the most sad or sacred experience in life. As much as we know everyone born of woman has a definite destiny with death, death and dying have from generation to generation, been cloaked in silence and mystery and few people ever want to address this topic until forced to do so by circumstances. Unfortunately, death is no respecter of persons and will catch up with the strong and the feeble, the old, the young and the unborn, the rich and the poor and makes its visits and harvest in all corners of the earth.

For believers, death is a brief separation from those that we love and cherish, but not the end. In John 11 verses 25-26 Jesus said "I am the resurrection and the life, those who believe in me, even though they die like everyone else, will live again. They are given eternal life for believing in me and will never perish." A human being has three dimensions – body, spirit and soul (mind, will and emotions). Paul says in 2 Corinthians 5:8 "Yes we are fully confident, and we would rather be away from these bodies, for then we will be at home with the Lord".

When someone's life is over in this world, the mortal body perishes. If they believed in Jesus Christ, though they are physically dead, they will live for ever in the spirit and also in our memories. Paul reminds us that "*To be absent from this body is to be present with the Lord*". For the initial grieving period, we will inevitably undergo emotional pain and grief. The intensity of our grief will vary from person to person; dependent on the relationship we had with the person who has passed away, their age and sometimes how they died. However, we gradually start adjusting to their absence from our lives, making small steps back and forth in our healing process. We begin to deal with their memories, retaining the good memories that will help you continue as best as is humanly possible, with your life. As much as is possible, try to discard those memories that bring back heartache from your past and may hinder your progress now or in the future. Unfortunately, you may have some unfinished issues that you might have to deal with before they can go away. Fond memories will help in your healing, especially any good plans you might have worked on together with your departed loved ones, e.g. with a spouse, with your parent(s), your siblings, your child or even a friend. At times, it might help to ask yourself, "How would (your loved one) want me to do with my life in their absence?" I doubt if anyone would want any of their surviving family to grieve for ever. Some have even said they would want the best for those surviving them, especially where long periods of major illnesses have preceded a death. The dying person has often been heard praying and hoping that their families and caregivers would learn to take care of themselves, do the things they have missed on like self grooming, going on a deserved holiday, going to church or visiting families near and far. Some have wished them just time to rest and enjoy themselves after all the care they have accorded them.

As believers, the Holy Bible reminds us in Jeremiah 1:5 "Before you were born I set you apart and appointed you s my spokesperson to the world". David also said that our days are numbered and God ***alone*** knows our end from the beginning. Whatever mode of death and time catches up with us might surprise us and our loved ones; but no death ever surprises our God and creator, whether early or late in life. Knowing that after death we will either go to heaven or hell might bring some kind of fear in people when death approaches us or our loved ones. But the good news is that Jesus Christ died on the cross to redeem each of us, paying in full the cost of our sins with his own cleansing blood, for us to have life and have it more abundantly, free from sin and death. In doing so, He secured an eternal life for all who believe in Him.

As a hospice/hospital chaplain, I have been blessed in experiencing the death of believers who knew fully well "where they were headed". While like everyone else they would be concerned with their survivor's" fate, more often than not, they die in peace. They die in great anticipation even in the midst of painful terminal illnesses, yearning and hungry for a better land and life where they will be free from their pain, sorrow and tears that was a part of their living for few or many years. Many are even able to boldly tell you what they are looking for in their next "home", like my own late mother who kept telling us that she could barely wait to get there and sing for the Lamb of God for ever. Some have actually been heard saying they are ready to go and that they see angels beckoning them. Others say they see their long gone parents, siblings or children. As much as they are concerned for those they will be leaving behind, they see death as an open door into a better and everlasting life.

On the contrary, I have seen some people on their dying bed suddenly gripped by great fear as they experience their bodies gradually declining and something tells them time is running out for them. Being critically ill, they suddenly face the reality of their eminent death and departure from this life. On several occasions, I have had the humbling experience of leading some to Christ at the last hour while they were scared and not sure that God would accept them because of the life they have led. To them death becomes a feared threat because of their uncertain future. For some to whom salvation has been offered and rejected in the past, they suddenly realize that a permanent and final transition is about to take place and ask how they can receive Christ's forgiveness and if God would still give them a chance. Some have changed their eternal home at the last hour while some have sadly missed out when death struck them suddenly or they lost their minds before deciding. But God in His infinite love stands watching and waiting till our last breath wanting to give us an eternity with him. He patiently waits to give everyone a chance to accept His gift of eternal life. Romans 6:23 says "For the wages of sin is death; but the free gift of God is eternal life through Christ Jesus our Lord".

It is a very comforting thing to know that our departed loved one walked with the Lord to the end, which also gives us a hope and desire to see them again in the heavenly home. Sadness and grief will still be there, but eased by that hope. Perhaps we too owe the same hope and gift to our own families and friends after we die like everyone else will.

Yes, death is definitely messy, painful and unbearable. It causes us to feel as if we are separated or alienated from God. It may also challenge our beliefs and bring a crisis in our faith. But for believers, there is something greater, beautiful and profound beyond pain and loss. There is HOPE. The Lord has promised to prepare a place in heaven above. This is a home where we will always be with him and those that we love dearly.

"I'm pressing on the upward way, new heights I'm gaining every day

Still praying as I'm onward bound, lord plant my feet on higher ground."

Philippians 4:14 challenges us to keep pressing on towards the prize of eternal life.

One of the hardest places and moments in life can be standing beside the bed either at home, hospital or wherever else, witnessing the death of a loved one. Even the thought of such a moment is itself very scary for many people, but it happens often. I have been called to be with families as the doctors turn off life support machines and other gadgets to let somebody's loved one pass on from this life to another in death. It may be from a terminal illness or after a fatal accident. This is a traumatic experience which only those who have experienced it can understand. The reality is that even when one has been sick for a long time and death was expected, it is always very difficult to let go. When families are asked by the doctors to give consent for them to turn off any life support, many are left with the guilt of letting go of their loved ones. This will be part of their healing needs in their grieving process.

Keeping a vigil when a loved one is dying is a very sacred experience when family members may gather to say their goodbyes and provide care to their loved one. All care at this point is now focused on keeping the patient as comfortable as possible, rather than treating medical conditions. But the thought of being present when someone is dying or taking their very last breath is scary to many people. Learning to recognize the signs of imminent death, knowing how to talk to the dying person, and knowing what to do after death occurs will help alleviate your fears and allow you to stay with your loved one through the closing of the circle of life and death. He/she may be communicating to the last minute while others are in a comma. It is said that even when they are in a comma and unresponsive, the last sense to go is hearing. We are therefore encouraged to say our goodbyes and assure them of our love now and always.

If possible and while your loved one is still able to hear and communicate with you, it is important to discuss any unfinished business, get them to tell you their personal wishes, especially, for after they are gone out of this life. It would be important to write down

some of these things especially where some family members live far away and may need to know the dying persons wishes and plans for her survivors. A living will outlining what they would like done or not done for them if they became critically ill and unable to communicate is very important. The presence of such instructions will alleviate misunderstandings between those left behind. It will also ensure that nothing is done to them in their dying moment that they did not want like codes and other very aggressive measures when the circumstances clearly indicate that they are not getting better. The absence of such written instructions leaves no choice but for the medical personnel to do whatever measures they deem necessary to keep the patient alive until their bodies give up. The worst thing is that it places traumatic and unpleasant responsibility on one's family at such times, putting them through experiences that might haunt them for the rest of their lives.

A written will instructing those who survive you on how your estate should be settled is of paramount importance. This too will take away the unnecessary misunderstandings among family members, which may unnecessarily affect their relations for many years to come. Aware that we all have a date with death, it is therefore important that as much as we can, we keep our "house" in order, especially if one has a family for whom we would like to leave a lasting legacy.

It is ironic that after all the struggles and efforts we undergo trying to make a name, wealth and so forth, the most important things are the "Precious Memories" that we leave behind to be passed down from one generation to another long after we are gone out of this life.

This may be a very appropriate time to share some five important things before it is too late.

> *"Please forgive me", "I forgive you", "Thank*
> *you", "I love you" and "Goodbye"*
> *(Ira Byrock – 1998)*

Death

I know little of what is on the other side of death, but I do know one thing, I know my Master is there, and that is enough"

A few months or years after we die, people may never remember how well we dressed, the kind of cars we drove or the earthly mansions we lived in. They will mostly remember the lasting impressions and impact we had on their lives – good or bad. It is a good time to repair our relationships – forgive and reconcile with each other. We need to pass on our blessings and personal stories. It would be nice to have lived a life that was like an arrow pointing them to Christ and the hope of glory, because there would be an anticipation of being reunited again.

3

What is Grief?

Grief is like a sudden, unexpected and unplanned journey with no road map or time to pack or psychologically prepare oneself. It is like suddenly having to jump out of a plane in a parachute without any warning. You have no idea where or how you will land and what life will be like if you survive and when you land wherever. It involves emotions, feelings and often times diverse physical reactions or symptoms. Grief takes you through unexpected places and uncharted territories, with feelings of never knowing what to expect at any given time. It is a multi-faceted response to loss. While grief is mostly viewed as an emotional response, it has other dimensions like physical, cognitive, behavioral, social and psychological issues. Grief is an emotionally wrenching experience filled with all kinds of vivid and contradictory feelings. Grief is therefore not just sadness, but many other things go with it. Grief is the feeling of reaching out to someone who has always been there, only to find when we desperately need them just once more, they are no longer there. It is however related to our self concept. Grief is often influenced by our attitudes and opinions, politics, religion and our philosophy of life. It is a stressful experience which can adversely affect one's health and life thereafter. Sometimes, many aspects of our background will affect or impact our grieving process like varied ethnic religious groups, each with their own rituals about death, different gender roles (male or female) may affect how we grieve. For example, most men may be reluctant to cry or show their emotions openly. Some people may want to visit the grave while others do not want to.

The first thing that is mostly thought of when the word "Grief" is mentioned anywhere is the loss to death of a loved one. Grief is a normal and natural response resulting in a conflicting mass of human emotion to any kind of loss that brings discomfort or major changes to one's life. There are many other un-acknowledged losses like divorce, broken relationships, loss of a new or long-held job, a major life changing terminal illness, relocation, retirement, diagnosis with a chronic illness, loss of a family home passed on from many generations, and many other kinds. It is more of a state of being than just emotions of sorrow, sadness and suffering. It also brings a deep sense of powerlessness, even hopelessness.

When grieving, one may even wish to skip the holiday gatherings. This is normal and okay. The sad thing is that we live in a world that has limited ability to talk openly and honestly about grief, resulting in isolation and loneliness for those grieving. Grief is almost always a taboo topic and we are mostly ill prepared and inadequately equipped to address it when death strikes. It is like a roller coaster of emotions. Unfortunately, we end up circulating lots of misinformation. By acting strong for our children, showing no feelings, we teach our children to do the same. In dealing with grief, there will be a wide variety of responses often influenced by people's personalities, family, culture, social habits and rules, spirituality, religious beliefs and practices, family traditions and protocol, step or extended families, separated/divorced families. Grief is not necessarily an enemy but also a friend that leads us into dealing with our loss and pain. However long the grieving process will take, it does get better and bearable gradually, allowing us to move on with life somehow. We often say *"It is in the valley of life that we learn the greatest lessons of life"*. With life comes the long difficult and painful process of finding and developing life beyond loss. Experiencing the grief and loss of a loved one is traveling into a valley like no other. The reality is that there is a valley between every mountain. Valleys are those dark experiences that strengthen our minds, teach us the greatest lessons of faith, strength and patience. But the most important and needed thing is the lesson of **HOPE**. Hope that gradually the high and low of life will become less intense. But it may take years to get over the loss. Hope encourages us to lean on God and allow him to carry us through our sorrow when nothing else is working to soothe our pain and anguish of loss. Paul reminds us in 1 Thessalonians 4:13-14 "Not to be full of sorrow like people who have no hope. For if we believe that Jesus died and was raised to life again, we also believe that when Jesus comes, God will bring back with Jesus all the Christians who have died"

WHAT IS BEREAVEMENT?

Unlike Grief which covers many diverse losses, bereavement is experienced at the death and loss of a loved one. Even though bereavement is a normal part of life for everyone who has survived the death of a loved one, be it a parent, sibling, child, spouse/partner, close friend or colleague, it carries a certain amount of risk if adequate support is not made available or sought. Some of the risks may include breakup of marriages, especially after the loss of a child, personal faith and belief system may be challenged; some mental illnesses can also be traced to have been triggered by the loss of a loved one.

It is not unusual to see a grieving person who has been so totally dependent on the deceased loved one, that when death strikes they feel completely incapacitated and loose all meaning to their own lives. Some end up suicidal or self destructive. It was at such a time that David confessed loosing hope and feeling paralyzed with fear (psalm 143:4) "I am losing all hope; I am paralyzed with fear". Some people may be able to process their bereavement gradually alone, but others would do better by seeking help from professional bereavement counselors to promote and help with the healing process. It would also be helpful if possible, to go for Grief counseling support groups either professionally or peer-led.

4

EXPERIENCING GRIEF AND BEREAVEMENT

In many parts of the world, it is viewed as a weakness to express or expose your grief or bereavement. While both of these experiences may linger on for months or even years for some people, society will predominantly hurry you up to "get over it" and "move on with life" like everyone. It is not unusual to see someone bury a parent, a child, a spouse or other family members and return to work immediately and stoically stand up strong and bold while their broken hearts are secretly bleeding and hurting so bad. Unless dealt with properly and gradually, if grief is suppressed, it is likely to explode somewhere in the near or distant future most unexpectedly in many forms. Some of them as drastically as going into serious bouts of depression, feeling suicidal or literary crumbling down emotionally, spiritually or even morally to the extent of needing hospitalization for safety and recovery. When we focus on the major tragedies affecting humanity in every corner of the universe, we can say there are so many "Sudden Deaths" of freedom, safety and control (by Russell Friedman and John W. James of the Grief Recovery Institute)

Normal Reactions to Grief vs. Myths about Grief:

It is very important to keep in mind always that grieving is a process or a journey and not a final event. In different countries, cultures and traditions, death, dying, grief and end of life mattes are approached with great apprehension. We all know that everyone who has a day when they were born must have a day when they will die. It does not matter whether one is dead just a few days, weeks or months after conception or over a hundred years, but as in every other aspect of life, whatever has a beginning has a definite end. The Egyptian Kings and others, prepared enormous and expensive burial places in pyramids, acknowledging that as rich and famous as they were, they knew that some day in their future they would die and leave this life.

It is therefore ironical that most people will talk and joke about everything in life but are not at all comfortable with the subject of death and whatever goes with it. It is for this reason that most people die without a will on their estate or even a living will to guide others on what they would want done for them in case of a serious illness where they can no longer express their wishes. In most cases, people behave as if not talking about death will keep it at a distance from us. But the bible tells us that God knows our end from the very beginning. David also prays that God would help us to know and realize that our days in life are numbered.

The reality and truth is that grief is a very personal experience where nobody can quite tell you how to process it. Yet in some cultures and countries there are set patterns of grieving. In many places, there are things "To do" and "Not to do". My experience is that when people tell you to stop weeping or crying in your grieving process, it is because you make them uncomfortable and they do not know how to handle you. Unaware of what is going on, they do this to take care of themselves and their discomfort around you, not necessarily for the grieving person who is weeping or crying. If one feels tearful, it is only fair to allow them to do what helps them best. Most people feel that tears are a sign of weakness. However, the truth is that crying in your grief is a very normal process that helps relieve one's feelings. There is nothing shameful about it and people should be allowed to do what helps them most, including weeping. Let us remember too that "Jesus Wept" when he learnt that His friend Lazarus had died. (John 11:35) When a death takes place in the family, a lot of people will try to keep the children from everything that is going on around the death. This is a sad way of dealing with it, especially if the child had a relationship or interaction with the deceased. They too have reason to walk through the grieving process, since they will inevitably notice the absence of this person from the family or close friends. It is important to include the children, using appropriate language and explanations of what is going on. This raises the need to keep the children informed when there is a serious illness in the family that may eventually result in death so that the children too will not be taken by surprise. This lays some necessary stepping stones for the adults when death strikes and one has to explain to the children what happened to their parent, grand parent, sibling or any other member of the family who dies. This also facilitates for the children to grow up aware that people die and we need to be careful how we relate with others while still alive.

Once death has taken a loved one, people become anxious and tense around the grieving families, not knowing what to say to comfort them without hurting them. In the process, some people will totally avoid discussing a loss with the grieving persons. Unfortunately, this might leave them feeling very lonely and isolated in the midst of many people. On the contrary, grieving persons normally appreciate friends willing to share the good memories of the deceased person and even talk about the pain that loss and grief has brought to this family. As friends and family do this with the grieving people, you help break the element of grief (the big elephant in the room) instead of going round and round about it without attacking it.

In many cases, the grieving person is so very afraid of moving on with life. The fear that they will be seen or experienced as abandoning or forgetting the deceased loved one. But this is not so because love will last beyond grief through one's commitment to living fully. Perhaps the deceased person would actually rejoice at seeing the grieving person picking up their broken pieces and the family baton, move on a step at a time, and be able to carry on the legacy they both worked on together. Moving on may not be automatic or easy, but it is worth the effort. The uniqueness of grief also encourages us to be open to those wanting to support and companion us through the grieving and mourning process. We will therefore need to tell people what kind of help we need most. Teach others about your loss and they will support you more effectively.

The most common way offered to deal with our grief is to try to move away from grief and hope it will go away quickly, but unfortunately, the more you suppress it the harder it will be when finally it catches up with you and explodes at the wrong time and places. Instead, one should move towards the pain, experience it and allow yourself all the space and time you need to handle it appropriately. Grief is not a matter of the head but of the heart.

It is hard to tell when one has finally gotten over their grief; even though we constantly hear others tell us to "Get Over" with the grief and move on with life. We cannot say it often enough that this too will vary from person to person. However, there are some things that will let you know how well or badly you are doing with your grief. It is important to watch out on this so that if your grief is prolonged and intensifying instead of subsiding, you can seek professional help to carry you over the hardest points. Here are just a few indicators of how well you are processing your grief:

- Life begins to have increased meaning and hope again.

- Your eating and sleeping habits stabilize.

- You are able to enjoy life, relax, read or sing without guilt

- You have new reasons to look forward into the future.

- You feel comfortable renewing old relationships or establishing new ones in the community or in your working place.

- You find it easier to adjust to new changes in life.

- You experience new aspects of growth as you gradually move from your bereavement period, confident that you have had adequate time grieving

- You finally acknowledge and accept your new identity (widow/widower/orphan etc) seeing it as a part of life from now on

- You gradually realize that you can never get over your grief, but you become reconciled with it and live on as best as you can.

- You are comfortable expressing the pain of your grief and not suppressing it.

STAGES AND PROCESS OF GRIEF:

Dr. Elizabeth Kubler-Ross and others have labeled this as a "Grief Cycle". The stages will not fall in the same manner or sequence for everyone since we all grief differently. The way different people grieve is also dependent on the relationship between the deceased and the grieving person(s). It may also depend on the age, the circumstances of death and numerous other dynamics. The sad reality is that we may have expected the death especially after long periods of sickness or terminal illness, but, we are still ill prepared for grief. There five commonly experience stages of grief:

1. <u>Denial:</u>

At the point of receiving news of a death, or being present with the dying person and experiencing them taking their last breath one may be overwhelmed by a sense of total disbelief. One may even hope that this is just a dream which will soon pass away and the deceased will still be alive and hopefully getting better if they have been sick. This may be so when the deceased has been sick for long, recovered and bloomed for a few days and then suddenly passes away when everyone assumed they were on their way to full recovery. This is a point and place in life where the grieving person is unable to come to terms with what has just happened to change their lives for ever. Some may intentionally keep themselves too busy taking care of "stuff", even acting as if nothing has happened and often tell you that they are doing "just fine". This often happens in the case of a spouse death where the widow or widower feels the need to be strong, protective and available to their children. It can also happen in the case of an eldest sibling/ eldest child (the family caregiver) in the loss of another sibling or any of their parents. They too will be too busy taking care of things, comforting and being strong for the other siblings or the surviving parent. They may keep themselves too busy with the funeral and other arrangements, taking no time to process their own grieving and face their own loss. It is important to allow yourself to experience the pain and not try to escape it by staying too busy or taking medication to numb your pain. A period of shock and denial can last from hours to days to months. The more traumatic and unexpected the death, the longer the shock may last. Suppressing your grief will only delay the grieving process and intensify the feelings. While working through the grief is the best thing, unfortunately it is one of the hardest things in life.

I was such a person after the sudden tragic motor vehicle accident death of my younger brother who followed me and my best friend. He left behind five children, the youngest only three weeks old and a young wife who was recovering from a cesarean section. As can be expected in the first family death of a young 40 years old professional son with great potential in whom the family had great dreams, many lives were shattered, especially that of my mother who never quite recovered until she died 14 years later. My younger siblings were all in great shock and disbelief. His wife and everyone else were all looking up to me as the eldest child in the family of 10 children, for emotional support and guidance. The other reason is that I was already in the counseling support ministry with my church. As best as I could, and with so many things to be taken care of and funeral arrangements to be made, I stayed calm, composed and on top of everything until a month after the funeral and everyone was processing their grief well. I guess when I noticed that everyone else was settling down and gradually moving on, and with some time and space to myself, it suddenly dawned on me that the brother and friend I used to turn to for emotional support was no longer there. A month from my brother's death I literary crumbled and landed in a hospital with severe back ache, complete emotional drain and a deep sense of loss and grief. I cried continuously and was inconsolable. Gradually, I came to terms with my loss and ganged up with my siblings and parents for comfort and survival through this major transition to a life without our brother. At this stage, shock is protective and enables us to grieve in our own way and comfortable pace.

Denial is a common reaction to almost everyone when we hear of a death. Our intervention in helping the grieving person should include providing a calm and reassuring presence, a quiet and soft atmosphere that allows the information to sink in gradually and pave way for the grieving process in a healthy way. It is hard and even unnecessary to force people out of this stage and the truth is that gradually reality will hit home. If the grieving person is hysterical, let them do it but remain present and visible, giving water, soft drinks, coffee a shoulder to lean on or whatever else they may need for support and comfort at that instance.

2. <u>Anger</u>

Depending on who is being mourned, anger may be manifested in many forms and against different people. Even in the case of believers, most often there is anger against God for not protecting their loved ones from maybe an accident, murder, or even for not healing them from a serious illness that might have claimed their life. Questions like "Why me, why now, why my son? Why would God allow such a cruel death" etc. will be prevalent even though no answers are available.

It may be in the case of a spouse whose passing away completely overturns the life of the surviving spouse. The husband who was the head of the family and navigated every aspect of his family's life as the main bread winner, is now suddenly and permanently taken away either in an accident, a sudden illness, a terminal illness, through a murder incident or has even taken his own life. Even though these are different causes of death, the surviving spouse might end up very angry at him now that she has to step into his very large shoes, minus his decision making role, protection and direction for the family. The family was so totally dependent on him, or maybe he controlled everything to the dot and the wife has a great challenge trying to find her way around life on her own, making a living, handling the children and paying their bills. She is suddenly thrown onto the fast moving wheel of life with no warning or preparation and feels overwhelmed or even threatened. She may also be angry at herself for not paying attention on how things were done. She may also get angry at her children who are suddenly looking up to her even for things their father did for them in his lifetime. The children may also be angry at having to live on without the protective father figure. The absence of the role model that he may have been is a scary thought. But more than anything having to readjust their lifestyle because a major life resource is suddenly missing is almost unimaginable.

A wife also dies leaving behind a young husband with young babies or children. Until her death, the wife planned all the household activities including grocery shopping, children's clothing or school needs. She supervised children's homework, attended their school events and took them for all doctor's appointments etc. She cooked, did laundry and planned all family celebrations and vacations since her husband was busy at work making a living for his family. Suddenly she passes away in an accident, at child-birth, or succumbs after a long battle with cancer or whatever else took her life. The husband is in a complete shock, almost in total disbelief that death has actually taken away the pillar of his family existence. He cannot imagine life for himself and their children without her and is beginning to feel cheated at the whole event. He might initially even be angry at God who seems not to care what will happen to his family or how he is expected to play the role of a mother and father all at once without any prior notice or preparation. The husband may even be angry at his deceased wife for leaving everything to him on top of his own previous heavy responsibilities. I can only imagine the kind of thoughts that cross his mind as well as those of their children towards a baby who is herself left behind at birth where the mother dies as a result of birthing complications. Perhaps this baby will experience anger and rejection from all angles as the cause of the mother's death unless the family is helped and supported from such a mind-set. The anger could even be projected against the medical personnel, his parents and other close relatives and friends offering to help. This can easily affect many other relationships and friends that were common to both who may be less and less available to the surviving family due to work and their own family responsibilities. The family ends up not only missing their mother or wife, but also her friends and sometimes relatives who visited mainly because of her. Anger may also result from the fact that they cannot comfortably participate in all the things that she usually initiated without the painful reminder of her absence. However, some people may find peace and comfort and visiting such places as a way of remaining connected to the deceased spouse or parent, doing the things they enjoyed doing together. Great care and support needs to be availed to the surviving family who may be initially be afraid of losing the only living memory of a departed spouse or parent in each other. This may be a very destructive stage of grief where the angry grieving person may be very rude and abrasive in language and reactions to anyone who comes too close to them. It is wisdom to give them some space, but not abandon them completely when they actually need help most. I'm reminded of Job's friends who came to comfort him (Job2:11-13), but seeing how deep his grief was, sat silently for seven days without saying a word. They represent the first chaplains or pastoral caregivers who gave a ministry of their presence until Job was comfortable enough to grieve outwardly in the open.

Intervention at this point may often be tough and complicated to help the grieving person(s). In our efforts to intervene and help, we must be careful not to be experienced as judging and least caring. One of the most supportive ways is to listen attentively and validate the reasons for the anger being projected instead of reacting harshly. While anger is often viewed as a bad reaction, it may at times be a gift and an expression of trust by the grieving person in that they can trust you with their emotions and your willingness to help where you can. In other incidences as in divorce, loss of a job and livelihood or a diagnosis of a terminal illness, anger may actually be projected to the least expected and closest family or friends. The best and most helpful gift to the grieving person(s) at this point may be your patience and silent compassion and not taking it personally. However, when anger becomes destructive, it may be necessary to set up boundaries to protect others who may be attacked unfairly or unexpectedly. "Time Out" may be necessary, explaining that while we are willing to help some changes are necessary for everyone's good before we can continue. If necessary, encourage the hostile grieving person to walk, jog, do some cleaning or watch a movie. Listening to some soothing and calm music might also help. Invite them also to come up with other activities that they know and enjoy that might help them deal with their grief and pain. We as the support system need to remember that acting up on our part will not help to quell the ongoing episodes. We may need to be tough and firm but cannot afford to be swallowed up in the anger.

3. <u>Bargaining</u>

This is the tough stage in which the grieving person bargains with God or whoever they see as their higher power. The terminally ill may be heard praying and pleading with God to give them a second chance with a promise that they would change their lives and live in obedience to God's laws and desires. They might even promise that they will serve in ministry of one kind or the other. It may be that those who are seriously sick as a result of some bad habits like smoking, drug and substance abuse and chemical dependency promise to discontinue all these if God heals them. Some may live to do this successfully while others will do so only for a little while before going back to the same habits that might eventually cost them their lives. The bargaining usually does not hold well for long and is not easily sustainable.

Like Hannah of the Bible, parents have been known to promise God the same that if He heals their sick children they will teach them to love and live for God if they get well. In journeying through abuse and battering in rocky marriages, the abused may also be promising God that if He saves their marriages, they will be better spouses and better role models for others struggling in similar situations. This often brings the abused to a grey area of living in denial and wishful thinking and bargaining. One may even end up hanging on a little too long under hostile brutalities, enduring un-necessary cruelty while hoping for a change of attitude in the abuser. Many times the end result has been death or deep emotional/physical wounds and scars that might otherwise have been avoided. During the bargaining stage, many different characters may be involved. Between couples who have been struggling in their relationships, either may be promising the other that things will improve if the other stopped drinking, recover from serious illness that may be threatening their marriage with death. The same may apply in parent child relationships. I have seen adult children who have for various reasons disconnected from their parents for long periods. Suddenly, they are summoned home because a parent is dying. Some have been heard dealing with guilt and regrets, bargaining and pleading with the dying parents that if they recover things will improve and the son or daughter will stay home to take care of them and sort out whatever had gone wrong between them. The sudden realization that death is really inevitable and there may never be another chance to make up with each other, often results in various family members being frantic and demanding that aggressive measures be taken to sustain a life that may well have already gone in a critical terminal illness, or other tragic life events. These may include fatal accidents, a heart attack or stroke, cancer etc, where nothing can be done to sustain the ending life. Those bargaining may appear to be the most caring or affected, but may actually be dealing with their own guilt, regrets and wishful thinking.

God You Said....

- Seek the Lord while He may be found, Call upon Him while He is near. *(Isaiah 55:6)*

The Lord is to be sought at all times by the Christian Entrepreneur. Seek for Him, and enquire after Him, as your portion and happiness; seek to be reconciled to Him and acquainted with Him, and to be happy in His favor. Be solicitous to find Him; take the appointed method of finding Him, making use of Christ as your way, the Spirit as your guide, and the word as your rule. Pray to Him, to be reconciled, and being reconciled, pray to Him for every thing else you have need of. Now His patience is waiting on us, His word is calling to us, and His Spirit striving with us. The Christian Entrepreneur should now improve their advantages and opportunities; for now is the accepted time.

God You Said....

- Now this is the confidence that we have in Him, that if we ask anything according to His will, He hears us. And if we know that He hears us, whatever we ask, we know that we have the petitions that we have asked of Him. *(1 John 5:14-15)*

The Lord Christ emboldens the Christian Entrepreneur to come to God in all circumstances, with all our supplications and requests. Through Him the Christian Entrepreneur petitions are admitted and accepted of God. It is important to know that the matter of the Christian Entrepreneur's prayer must be agreeable to the declared will of God. It is not fit that the Christian Entrepreneur should ask for or pray for what is contrary either to His majesty and glory or to Christian Entrepreneurs own good, who are His and dependent on Him. If the Christian Entrepreneur's prayer is in line with God's will, he or she may have confidence that their prayer of faith shall be heard in heaven and they can know that their petitions, which are heard, will be answered.

God You Said….

- Then you will call upon Me and go and pray to Me, and I will listen to you. And you will seek Me and find Me, when you search for Me with all your heart. *(Jeremiah 29:12)*

The Christian Entrepreneur must have a quest for God that includes a level of intensity beyond what might be termed ordinary prayer. The word "search" along with the phrase "with all your heart" suggests an earnestness that borders on desperation. The word "search" suggests a "following after," or close pursuit of a desired objective; it also implies a diligence in the searching process. To the Christian Entrepreneur this means pursuing God in prayer until your desired objective is accomplished, which is to have a successful Christian Business that would stand the test of time.

God You Said….

- But you beloved, building yourselves up on your most holy faith, praying in the Holy Ghost. *(Jude 20)*

Here the Christian Entrepreneur is exhorted to preserving constancy in truth and holiness. The way to hold fast your confession is to hold on to it. Having laid your foundation well in a sound faith, and a sincere upright heart, the Christian Entrepreneur must build upon it, making further progress continually. When praying in the Holy Ghost, the Christian Entrepreneur must know that prayer is the nurse of faith; the way to build up ourselves in our most holy faith is to continue instant in prayer, Romans 12:12 says "continuing steadfastly in prayer." The Christian Entrepreneur prayers will prevail when they pray in the Holy Ghost, that is, under the Holy Ghost guidance and influence, according to the rule of His word, with faith, fervency, and constant persevering.

God You Said….

- This book of the Law shall not depart from your mouth, but you shall meditate in it day and night, that you may observe to do according to all that is written in it. For then you will make your way prosperous and then you will have good success. *(Joshua 1:8)*

To enjoy the prosperity and be successful, the Christian Entrepreneur must do three things with regard to the scriptures: (1). The scriptures must not depart from the Christian Entrepreneurs mouth; they must talk about them; (2). The Christian Entrepreneur must meditate on them day and night, to think about them constantly; (3). The Christian Entrepreneur must do everything written in them, to obey its commands fully and to act on them. The Christian Entrepreneur who is obedient to God will lack no manner of thing that is good.

God You Said....

- For assuredly, I say to you, whoever says to this mountain, Be removed and be cast into the sea, and does not doubt in his heart, but believes that those things he says will be done, he will have whatever he says. Therefore I say to you, whatever things you ask when you pray, believe that you receive them and you will have them. *(Mark 11:23-24)*

For the Christian Entrepreneur, a mountain is symbolic of an obstacle, hindrance, or insurmountable problem. The Christian Entrepreneur has to know that faith is the key that releases the resources of heaven into their situation. In verse 24, Jesus uses a hyperbole (a deliberate exaggeration of speech or writing used for effect) here to stress the importance and power of faith. The Christian Entrepreneurs faith has to be in Christ Jesus. This type of faith is only achieved through constant prayer.

God You Said....

- Be anxious for nothing, but in everything by prayer and supplication, with thanksgiving, let your requests be made known to God; and the peace of God, which surpasses all understanding, will guard your hearts and minds through Christ Jesus. *(Philippians 4:6-7)*

Here the Christian Entrepreneur cannot be anxiously solicitous; let what will occur; because anxiety cannot change the state or condition of anything from bad to good, but will infallibly injure your own souls. God alone can help you; He is disposed to do it, but you must ask by prayer and supplication; without this He has not promised to help you. Supplication means continuance in earnest prayer. With thanksgiving means thanking God for the innumerable favors already received for you and your business; also for the dangers, evils, and deaths turned aside.

The scripture goes on to say "and the peace of God", which is the harmonizing peace of all your passions and appetites which is produced by the Holy Spirit, and arises from a sense of pardon and the favor of God; "shall guard your hearts", which is saying that the Christian Entrepreneurs heart shall be kept in a strong place or castle. The Christian Entrepreneurs heart is the seat of all their affections and passions, "and minds", which is your understanding, judgment, and conscience. All of this shall be kept "through Christ Jesus", by whom you were brought into this state of favor, through whom you are preserved in it, and in whom you possess it; for Christ keeps that heart in peace in which He dwells and rules. This peace surpasses all understanding; it is of a very different nature from all that can arise from human occurrences; it is a peace which Christ has purchased, and which God dispenses; it is felt by all the truly men and women of God, but can be explained by none; it is communion with the Father, and His Son Jesus Christ, by the power and influence of the Holy Spirit. The Christian Entrepreneur must rest in this peace.

Things To Remember

1. Commit yourself to daily communications with the Holy Spirit through prayer. Your relationship will be enhanced immeasurably.

2. Set realistic goals for yourself. Do not try to set up a monk-like routine if you have not previously incorporated prayer into your life. It takes twenty-one days to create a new habit. If you can pray ten minutes a day for twenty-one days, you can establish the habit of prayer.

3. Find a quiet time for prayer. Once you have established the time, stick to it.

4. Give thanks for all things, even for those things that have not yet been manifested. You will discover that prayers are often answered before they are even asked.

5. Remember that prayer is energy and follows universal laws.

Chapter 3

THE CHRISTIAN ENTREPRENEUR & FAITH

For the Christian Entrepreneur, to have faith is to believe in something or someone, to fully trust, to be so confident that you base your actions on what you believe. Faith in God then, is having the kind of trust and confidence in God and in Christ that leads you to commit your whole soul, your whole being, your whole business, all your gifts, talents and abilities to Him as Saviour, Lord, Master and King.

The NIV translation says, "Faith is being sure of what we hope for, and certain of what we do not see." (Hebrews 11:1 NIV).

The NKJV of the Bible says, "Now faith is the substance of things hoped for, the evidence of things not seen." (Hebrews 11:1).

Faith is a spiritual substance. When you have this spiritual substance in you, it communicates to you a certain inner knowing that the thing you are hoping for, such as success in your business, is certainly established, even before you see any material evidence that it has happened.

Faith is a spiritual force. Faith in God is a response to God's Word which moves God to act. Jesus said in Mark 11:23, "For assuredly I say to you, whoever says to this mountain, 'Be removed and cast into the sea,' and does not doubt in his heart, but believes that those things he says will be done, he will have whatever he says." Words mixed with the real, pure faith can and will move mountains or any other problem that the Christian Entrepreneur may face.

Faith in God must be from the heart. It is not merely intellectual. It is spiritual. "For with the heart one believes unto righteousness, and with the mouth confession is made unto salvation." (Romans 10:10)

Faith causes you to know in your heart before you see with your eyes. "For we walk by faith, not by sight." (2 Corinthians 5:7)

Some say, "seeing is believing." Once you see the thing hoped for already existing in the natural order, you don't need faith.

Hope is a condition for faith. Hope is "a positive unwavering expectation of good." Hope is for the mind (1 Thessalonians 5:8; Hebrews 6:19), an anchor for the soul. It keeps us in the place where we can believe, but it is not in itself "faith". Yet, without hope there are no "things hoped for", and therefore there cannot be faith.

Through faith we can know we have the answer to our prayer before we see anything change in the natural order (1 John 5:14,15). Jesus said, "Therefore I say to you, whatever things you ask when you pray, believe that you receive them, and you will have them." (Mark 11:24). God expects us, even commands us, to believe that our petitions are answered by God at the moment we make them. We must believe that the response is immediately sent when we pray. Faith is like the confirmation slip in our hearts that the goods are on the way. We have that confirmation slip instantly from God. We sense it in our hearts. The manifestation of those goods, the answer received, comes later as long as we are patient and do not throw away our confidence. (Hebrews 10:35-39; Hebrews 6:12)

Living faith always has corresponding actions. We talk what we really believe, and we act according to what we really believe. The heroes of faith like Abraham were considered men of faith because they acted on what God showed them. They acted on their faith. (Hebrews 11:17-38, James 2:21-23).

Why We Must Believe God
Hebrews 11:6 says, "But without faith it is impossible to please God, for he who comes to God must believe that He is, and that He is a rewarder of those who diligently seek Him."

"Whatever is not of faith is sin" (Romans 14:23) and God hates sin. When we don't believe God, we treat Him like He is a liar. Remember that He is everywhere and sees all things. He is hurt when we act like He doesn't exist, or that He will not do what He promised to do. Only when we have confidence in God and His Word can we please Him.

Lack of faith leads to lack of obedience. God's commands can only really be fulfilled through faith. Without confidence in God's promises a man will never really do what God says. Lack of obedience in God's eyes is rebellion. Such lack of obedience dishonors God and surely deserves to be punished.

"The just shall live by faith" (Romans 1:17). We must live by faith in order to be considered by God "right" and "correct". Otherwise we stand condemned.

Those who don't believe God inevitably believe in something else. God is not impressed. "Professing to be wise, they became fools." (Romans 1:22) In fact, those who don't fully believe God end up believing the devil somewhere along the track. It is very possible to believe what the devil says without even believing that he exists! Satan is speaking through so many philosophies and religions without openly declaring himself. Not too many actually know they are trusting the words of satan and his demons.

God is therefore righteous in expecting us to believe in Him and what He says. Who is better qualified to tell us the truth and help us to find answers for life and eternity?

Benefits of Faith

The Bible teaches us that genuine faith is "more precious than gold that perishes" (1 Peter 1:7). Indeed such faith is going to be "tested by fire". You can expect difficulties and persecutions in your life of faith, as well as blessings. Therefore to encourage you to hold onto and develop your faith, let's consider some of the benefits of faith.

1. Faith brings **salvation.** (Ephesians 2:8,9). Whoever believes in Him has eternal life (John 3:16), and shall not come into judgment, but

has passed from death to life (John 5:24). The just shall live by faith (Romans 1:17).

2. Faith brings answers to **prayer.** "And whatever_things you ask in prayer, really believing, you will receive." (Matthew 21:22). Since God tells us to pray for our daily bread (Matthew 6:11), faith is therefore a key to our material provision.

3. Faith brings all the benefits of salvation into our lives (Ephesians 2:8,9). This includes healing, prosperity, peace, love, joy (1 Peter 1:8), deliverance from demons and the curse, sanctification of the mind and emotions (the salvation of the soul) and any other benefit which the word of God promises to us.

4. Faith is a spiritual force through which our ministry for Christ in the marketplace becomes effective. (Mark 11:23; Matthew 17:19,20). The Christian Entrepreneur must know that faith is a major key to their entrepreneurial success. It brings to you what you need for your ministry, which is the marketplace and by imparting it to others (faith) through your life and your ministry of God's word, you enable the marketplace to receive the blessings of God's grace mentioned above.

5. In particular, faith is the major key for an effective healing and deliverance ministry which is needed in the marketplace. Jesus Christ "the same yesterday, today and forever" lives in the Christian Entrepreneur, and through the Christian Entrepreneur wants to reveal the power of salvation to men in a way they can see and feel. In this way, the Christian Entrepreneurs evangelism concerning the Kingdom of God will not be in talk, but in power (1 Corinthians 4:20).

How to Develop Faith

We see how important faith is. Yet some Christian Entrepreneurs despair here, thinking that they don't have faith. Yet faith comes (Romans 10:17), it can grow and develop. If you are not full of faith today, that doesn't mean you will be that way all your life. You can choose to be a Entrepreneur of faith!

Here are some keys to developing faith:

1. Listen to the Word of God as much as possible. "Faith comes by hearing, and hearing by the Word of God" (Romans 10:17). Constant attention to the Word of God produces faith, especially if we attend to it with an open heart and mind. The book of Proverbs encourages us to constantly keep the Word in our hearts and to keep our attention on it (Proverbs 4:20-22). Health is one of the benefits promised. What we listen to affects what we believe. If we listen to the TV more than to the Word, we will believe the lies of the world more than we will believe what God says. Constant attention to lies produces deception. Eventually the mind will accept something if that thing is heard often enough and persuasively enough. That is why we should keep hearing the Word of God, through preaching, Christian tapes, confession of the Word, daily fellowship with godly Christians. This will cause us eventually to believe the truth from our hearts.

2. Realize that every Christian Entrepreneur has been given a measure of faith by God. (Romans 12:3). We just have to use and develop what God has given. We must put it into action.

3. Pray in tongues and be full of the Spirit (Jude 20). If you have been baptised in the Spirit as the disciples were in the book of Acts, you should pray and praise in tongues often because through this you "edify yourself" (1 Corinthians 14:4) and "build yourself up in your most holy faith". Praying in tongues is a key to being full of the Spirit. Since faith is a fruit of the Spirit, all things are related together.

4. Obey God and the conviction of the Holy Spirit. It is as you walk that you gain strength. God will not reveal greater things to you until you are faithful in the things He is showing you NOW. Therefore obedience to the Spirit and what He is showing you through the Word or through your conscience is important in the development of your faith. You cannot have living faith without taking some practical steps of obedience. Act on what God is saying!

5. Give thanks. Give thanks for the results before you see them. Don't complain - that shows you doubt God's love and God's answer to your situation. Give thanks in all situations (1 Thessalonians 5:18).

6. Develop a life of praise and worship. Praise drives the powers of darkness away and brings the throne of God into your circumstances. Praising God is an act of faith and helps your faith to grow. It is commanded (Hebrews 13:15). Worship is admiring God through the Spirit. If you can perceive who is God, His power, His faithfulness and His love, your trust and faith in Him will grow.

7. Spend as much time as you can with people of faith. The spirit of faith on them will touch your life also (Proverbs 13:20).

8. Speak the Word. By saying with your mouth you exercise your faith, you hear the Word and you build it into your life. God's Word is anointed and has power when it is spoken to change the spiritual atmosphere (Joshua 1:8; Romans 10:10). Confession of God's Word (saying the same thing as God's word) brings you into the place where the Lord will move to fulfill it (Hebrews 3:1). The angels hearken to the voice of God's Word (Psalms 103:20).

9. Seek holiness, purity of heart. "Pursue peace with all men, and holiness, without which no one will see the Lord." (Hebrews 12:14). It is with the heart that man believes (Romans 10:10). To the extent that the heart has uncleanness, unforgiveness and other bad conditions within, the man will lose the spiritual perception of the Lord which enables his heart to believe. Purity and faith feed each other.

10. Remember that faith works by love (Galatians 5:6). The centurion (Matthew 8:5-13) and the woman of Canaan (Matthew 15:21-28) were both motivated by their love for another in coming to Jesus. And both were described as having great faith. Let us believe God for others to be blessed, in a spirit of love, and as we give of ourselves God will give blessings to us also (Luke 6:37). This is related to the idea of "seed-faith". Express your faith by planting a seed in terms of

some form of giving. God will release a multiplied harvest in return if we endure and do not faint (Hebrews 10:36).

God talks in faith. God "gives life to the dead and calls those things which do not exist as though they did" (Romans 4:17). Through faith-filled words, God created the universe (Hebrews 11:3). As sons of God we are called to be imitators of God, filled with God's Spirit (Ephesians 5:1,18).

When we are in Christ and we have the promise of God, we have the right to speak about something God has promised as if it existed even before our natural senses are conscious of it. It is our faith that gives substance to this confession of things not seen. For example, if we have believed God for a car, we can talk about our car before we see it. We should realize that God has already "given us all things that pertain to life and godliness" (2 Peter 1:3) and all spiritual blessings (Ephesians 1:3). But the effective receiving depends on our faith. Faith is confident of the faithfulness of God in His declared promises and talks and acts so, even before the natural eye sees.

Acting in Faith

Real faith has corresponding actions. Looking at Hebrews 11:4-37 we see that all those who are commended for their faith did something as well. It is possible to have actions, even religious actions, without real faith - but these actions are dead works. Without faith you can't please God. (Hebrews 11:6).

Sometimes confusion arises in this matter of faith and works. There is a radical difference between works or actions that spring from real faith, and works which spring from **Self** in an effort to earn God's approval. The former cannot be separated from real faith. The latter are as filthy rags to God (Isaiah 64:6), and are wrong because the man occupied with them cannot understand or accept God's free grace - that it is by Grace, by Christ that we are saved, and not by our own works.

Faith hears the word of God, the voice of God and acts in obedience with a trusting heart. God often speaks to us through our consciences by His Spirit, pressing us towards a particular kind of action which is based on God's Word. Real faith yields to God's suggestion and does it.

Jesus told the blind man to go to the pool to wash. The blind man, by acting in obedience to Jesus' words BEFORE he received healing, demonstrated the kind of faith which God required of him in that situation, and he was healed. (John 9:7). If he had not obeyed, he would not have been healed.

God told Abraham to offer his son Isaac up as a sacrifice. Abraham's obedience in this matter demonstrated the reality of his faith. (James 2:20-24). Even justifying faith is not passive. It does not rest in sin. Justifying faith works with repentance to open the door for the receiving of God's great salvation.

Overcoming the Enemies of faith

1. Ignorance. You cannot believe a promise until you hear it or find it. Much unbelief rises out of the fact that the Christian Entrepreneur just don't know what the Bible says. The cure for this is study, meditation and consideration of the Word.

2. Unbelief. This is the sinful choice to not believe God. It is usually motivated by pride, rebellion and ignorance. The cure for this is therefore to humble oneself, change one's mind, choose to believe. Fasting puts down the flesh and is often very effective in destroying the power of unbelief, because it aids in humbling ourselves and in removing fleshly distractions to the voice of God. If done correctly it can help us to focus on God and will make the spiritual things more intense to us, thereby destroying unbelief.

3. Fear. Negative fear is a negative emotion based on the real expectation of bad things to come. It is rooted in anxiety and a lack of trust in God's fatherly protection and love. Perfect love casts out fear. (I John 4:18). God is perfect love. Therefore by seeking God, His presence and the fullness of His Spirit we will be set free from fear. When we are conscious of God's power it is very easy to be courageous and bold. We expect success when we are consciously full of God and know that we are doing what He is telling us to

do. For the Christian Entrepreneur to overcome fear he or she must look to God and not to natural considerations which could cause our failure if God were not with us. Peter, looking to the wind and the waves, was overcome by a fear which paralyzed his faith and caused him to sink. He needed to keep looking to Jesus. God says, "Fear not, For I Am With You." (Isaiah 43:5). God gives us a reason not to fear, and a commandment. To fear anyone or anything except the Lord is a sin. We can overcome this sin by being full of God and looking to Him for success in our business.

4. Doubt. Doubt is an enemy to faith because it speaks with a voice that challenges the truth or the reliability of the word, which the Christian Entrepreneur should be believing. To overcome doubt we must fill ourselves with the Word of God, meditating deeply and repetitively on it. Doubt is the evidence of an **unconsecrated heart** and mind. It is the evidence of lack of devotion to God's Word. Doubt, like fear, torments. We must forgive others and give our whole hearts to God. We must stop listening to the voice of demons or the voice of our own carnal mind trained from early days to resist God. This is a decision for the Christian Entrepreneur. It helps to hear the testimonies of other Christian Entrepreneurs to overcome doubt. However, doubt will never be fully overcome until we, the Christian Entrepeneur treat the Bible as God's voice to us.

5. Discouragement. Sometimes we feel discouraged because of physical or emotional weakness or tiredness. We may be disappointed by the set backs in our business. We may be discouraged by the persecution of others, even of our families. Perhaps we have waited for what may or may not be God's promise to us, and we grow impatient. Many Christian Entrepreneurs at some time in their life become disappointed with God. Satan uses discouragement to weaken and if possible destroy our faith. To overcome discouragement we must make a decision to be strong in the Lord (Hebrews 12:12; Ephesians 6:10). We must want to be strong and stop making excuses for our weaknesses and failures. We must consider God's faithfulness to us in the past, even through difficulties (Hebrews 10:32-34). We must rededicate ourselves to God's Word, to thankfulness, to prayer and to the voice of the Spirit. We need to learn to obey the Spirit

in small things. Sometimes even great men of God like Elijah were discouraged. At one time, even after a great victory, he ran away from Jezebel, the witch. God restored Elijah through the ministry of angels, through his voice, and by getting him occupied in new missions. God is calling all of us to put our faith in action in many ways. True faith will lead the Christian Entrepreneur to stand on God's word.

God You Said….
- Blessed is the man who trusts in the Lord, and whose hope is the Lord. For he shall be like a tree planted by the waters, which spreads out its roots by the river, and will not fear when heat comes; but its leaf will be green, and will not be anxious in the year of drought, nor will cease from yielding fruit. *(Jeremiah 17:5-8)*

The Christian Entrepreneur who trusts in the Lord will have abundant strength, not only for their own business, but even for the needs of others.

The benefits here for the Christian Entrepreneur is:
1. God will plant your business in the right place.

2. Life giving resources are available; there will always be provision to run your business.

3. Fear is banished.

4. Your business will be sustained in the worst situations.

5. Fruit-bearing never ceases.

God You Said….
- And when He had come into the house, the blind men came to Him. And Jesus said to them, "Do you believe that I am able to do this?" They said to Him, "Yes, Lord." Then He touched their eyes, saying, "According to your faith let it be to you." *(Matthew 9:28-29)*

These blind men were persistent. They went right into the house where Jesus was staying. They knew Jesus could heal them, and they would let nothing stop them from finding Him. That's real faith in action. If you believe Jesus is the answer to your every need, don't let anything or anyone stop you from reaching Him.

God You Said....

• So Jesus said to them, because of your unbelief; for assuredly, I say to you, if you have faith as a mustard seed, you will say to this mountain, move from here to there, and it will move; and nothing will be impossible for you. *(Matthew 17:20)*

The Christian Entrepreneur needs to understand that faith that appears small or weak to us still can accomplish the humanly impossible (run a multi-million dollar business). This mountain was a figure for an obstacle, hindrance, or humanly insurmountable problem-none of which is impossible for God to deal with through committed people who accurately understand their authority and know His power, will, purposes, and provision.

The Christian Entrepreneur has to know when you plant a seed, such as starting a business, going out to look for new customers, looking for a new location, putting an employment ad in the paper looking for employees, etc., that God changes the nature of that seed so that it becomes a plant, and the power of life surges in that tender young plant to such a great extent that even a mountain of earth cannot stop it from pushing upward! Jesus says our faith in God is like a seed. When we put our faith into action, that is, when we release it to God, it takes on a totally new nature. It takes on the nature of a miracle in the making and that miracle will be a successful business.

God You Said....

• And we desire that each one of you show the same diligence to the full assurance of hope until the end, that you do not become sluggish, but imitate those who through faith and patience inherit the promises. *(Hebrews 6:11-12)*

Here hope keeps the Christian Entrepreneur from becoming lazy or feeling bored. Like an athlete, train hard and run well, remembering the reward that lies ahead.

God You Said....

- Therefore do not cast away your confidence, which has great reward. *(Hebrews 10:35)*

Hebrews 10:35 reminds the Christian Entrepreneur not to cast away his confidence, regardless of what it looks like in his or her business affairs, because by you holding on to your confidence in the midst of trials, will lead to a great reward. This should be exciting to the Christian Entrepreneur, God has promised you success. Psalm 37:4 states that "If you delight yourself in the Lord, He will give you the desires of your heart."

God You Said....

- But without faith it is impossible to please Him, for he who comes to God must believe that He is, and that He is a rewarder of those who diligently seek Him. *(Hebrews 11:6)*

Nothing so pleases God as a steadfast faith in all that He is and promises to do. The Christian Entrepreneur can be confident that God rewards those who diligently seek Him.

God You Said....

For My thoughts are not your thoughts, nor are your ways My ways, says the Lord, For as the heavens are higher than the earth, so are My ways higher than your ways, and My thoughts than your thoughts. *(Isaiah 55:8-9)*

The Christian Entrepreneur is encouraged to continue to seek the mind of the Lord while running his or her business. The scripture clearly states that His thoughts are higher than our thoughts and His ways are higher than our ways. God is reminding us that His plans transcend man's; man cannot always accurately read Gods' ways, nothing can stop His decrees.

God You Said....

* Now the just shall live by faith, but if anyone draws back, My soul has no pleasure in him. *(Hebrews 10:38)*

The Christian Entrepreneur has been justified since the death of Jesus Christ. Scriptures teaches that the just or justified shall live by faith. As Christian Entrepreneurs, we have no other option but to stand on the word of God. Ephesians 6:13-17 states that "and having done all, to stand. Stand therefore, having girded your waist with truth, having put on the breastplate of righteousness, and having shod your feet with the preparation of the gospel of peace; above all, taking the shield of faith with which you will be able to quench all the fiery darts of the wicked one. And take the helmet of salvation, and the sword of the Spirit, which is the word of God. In essence we have to "stand there for what we are standing there for."

The Christian Entrepreneur cannot draw back on what God has promised. James 1:6-8 states that "But let him ask in faith, with no doubting, for he who doubts is like a wave of the sea driven and tossed by the wind. For let not that man suppose that he will receive anything from the Lord; he is a double-minded man, unstable in all his ways". In essence, the just are those in right relationship with God. Their way of life is determined by their faith.

God You Said....

Now faith is the substance of things hoped for, the evidence of things not seen. (*Hebrews 11:1*)

The Christian Entrepreneur has to understand that faith is established conviction concerning things unseen and settled expectation of future reward. You have to know that your business is going to be successful, you have to know that your business is going to be around forever, you have to know that you are laying up wealth for your children's children. Here the Greek word translated substance literally means "a standing under" and was used in the technical sense of "title deed" the root idea is that of standing under the claim to the property to support its validity. Thus, faith is the title deed of things hoped for.

God You Said....
• "Lord, I believe, help my unbelief!" *(Mark 9:24)*

There will be times in the Christian Entrepreneurs life that unbelief will set in and the Christian Entrepreneur will have to disown it and wrestle with it. He or she will have to appeal to Christ for help.

God You Said....
• For as the body without the spirit is dead, so faith without works is dead also. *(James 2:26)*

The point of this analogy between the body and one's faith is that both require an energizing element. The absence of that element renders the other component dead. Faith inevitably calls the Christian Entrepreneur forward to action, to work within faith.

God You Said....
• Thus also faith by itself, if it does not have works, is dead. But someone will say, "You have faith, and I have works." Show me your faith with your works, and I will show you my faith by my works. *(James 2:17-18)*

The Christian Entrepreneur in running his or her business needs to understand that "their works show the genuineness of what they profess". Faith without works is dead.

God You Said....
• My brethren, count it all joy when you fall into various trials, knowing that the testing of your faith produces patience, but let patience have its perfect work that you may be perfect and complete lacking nothing. *(James 1:2-5)*

Becoming an Entrepreneur does not automatically exclude you from difficulties. The proper attitude in meeting adversity is to count it all joy, which is not an emotional reaction but a deliberate intelligent appraisal of the situation from God's perspective, viewing trials as a means or moral and spiritual growth. We do not rejoice in the trials themselves, but in their possible results. Testing carries the idea of proving genuineness. Trials serve as a discipline to purge faith of dross, stripping away what is false. Patience is not a passive resignation to adverse circumstances, but a positive steadfastness that bravely endures.

God You Said....

- Do you see that faith was working together with his works, and by works faith was made perfect? *(James 2:22)*

There is a practical harmony or synergism between vertical faith in God and horizontal works to a needy world. Faith is both spiritual and practical. Faith creates works and works perfect faith.

God You Said....

- Let us hold fast the confession of our hope without wavering, for He who promised is faithful. *(Hebrews 10:23)*

Hold fast is literally "hold down" It speaks of a firm hold which masters that which is held. Holding on is the human side of eternal security. The Reformers called it "the perseverance of the saints." It is not something we do to keep ourselves saved, but it is evidence, on the human side, that we are saved. For the Christian Entrepreneur, he or she has to hold down firmly what God has given them for their business. God would not have you start a business to fail.

How sad that many come to Christ and say they believe and yet are gone so soon. In the parable of the sower, Jesus illustrated four different kinds of response to the gospel. Some people are so far from wanting salvation that the devil simply takes away the seed of God's Word before it has time to germinate at all. Others respond joyfully at hearing the Word, but their "belief" lasts only until the first temptation. Still others believe until they run into a few problems. True believers, however, "are the ones who have heard the word in an honest and good heart, and hold it fast, and bear fruit with perseverance" (Luke 8:15). He who has begun a good work in you, is faithful to complete it unto the day of Jesus Christ. *(Philippians 1:6)*

God You Said….

- He will not allow your foot to be moved; He who keeps you will not slumber. *(Psalm 121:3)*

The key word for the Christian Entrepreneur in Psalm 121:3 is the Hebrew verb "shamar" which occurs six times in eight verses in Psalm 121, translated "keep", once as "protect" and once as "guard". Shamar conveys the picture of one exercising great care to watch over and so to keep, preserve, protect and guard. The Christian Entrepreneur has to know and have the faith to believe that God is preserving them, protecting them and guarding their businesses everyday and know that "no weapon formed against thee shall prosper".

God You Said….

- That the genuineness of your faith, being much more precious than gold that perishes, though it is tested by fire, may be found to praise, honor, and glory at the revelation of Jesus Christ. (*1 Peter 1:7)*

The Christian Entrepreneur must remember and understand that as he or she endures suffering, that their faith is being refined as with fire. They must value your faith more than gold. They must look forward to the coming of Jesus, so that their faith, having been tested, will result in praise, honor, and glory to Jesus.

God You Said….

- Jesus said to him, "If you can believe, all things are possible to him who believes." (*Mark 9:23)*

If thou canst believe. This was an answer to the request; and there was a reference in the answer to the doubt in the man's mind about the power of Jesus. I can help him. If THOU canst believe, it shall be done. Jesus here demanded faith or confidence in His power of healing. So He demands faith of every Christian Entrepreneur that comes to Him; and none that come without confidence in Him can obtain the blessing.

All things are possible to him that believeth. All things can be effected or accomplished--to wit, by God--in favour of him that believes; and if thou canst believe, this will be done. God will do nothing in the Christian Entrepreneur's favour without faith. It is right that we should have confidence in Him; and if we have confidence, it is easy for Him to help us, and He willingly does it. In our weakness, then, we should go to God our Saviour; and though we have no strength, yet He can aid us, and He will make all things easy for us.

God You Said....

• So then faith comes by hearing, and hearing by the word of God. *(Romans 10:17)*

The essence of faith consists in believing and receiving what God has revealed to you, and may be defined as that trust in the God of the Scriptures and in Jesus Christ whom He has sent, which receives Him as Lord and Savior and impels to loving obedience and good works. True faith includes at least three main elements (1) firm persuasion or firm conviction, (2) a surrender to that truth and (3) a conduct emanating from that surrender. In sum, faith shows itself genuine by a changed life and a changed belief system. The Christian Entrepreneur is destined to succeed as long as he or she stay true to God's word.

Things To Remember

1. Faith is the ability to not panic.

2. When we get tangled up in our problems, be still. God wants us to be still so He can untangle the knot.

3. Surviving and living your Entrepreneurial life successfully requires courage.

4. The goals and dreams you're seeking require courage and risk taking.

At the end of the day, you must have faith in yourself to change the things that need to be changed. No matter what is happening in your business, understand that things will change. Many have to remember this daily. The idea is not to live in or for the future, but to remember no one really knows what is to come. If you are having a difficult time in your business, have faith that it won't be forever. If you are not in the middle of a difficult time, be ready when things go wrong, and always have faith that they will get better.

Chapter 4

THE CHRISTIAN ENTREPRENEUR & DILIGENCE

Diligent means - steady in application to business; constant in effort or exertion to accomplish what is undertaken; assiduous; attentive; industrious; not idle or negligent.

Diligence is conscientiousness in paying proper attention to a task; giving the degree of care required in a given situation; persevering determination to perform a task; application: a diligent effort; vigilant activity; attentiveness; or care. Attentive and persistent in doing a thing; steadily applied; active; sedulous; laborious; unremitting; untiring.

The attention and care required of a person in a given situation; the opposite of NEGLIGENCE .

Diligence is the skill that a good businessperson exercises in his or her specialty. Diligence is the one key ingredient that all successful men and women share. Successful people never quit, they press on against all odds to claim the prize they seek. A diligent person starts working right away. A diligent person works hard to finish a job and do it well.

Proverbs 13:4 says, "The sluggard [lazy person] craves and gets nothing, but the desires of the diligent are fully satisfied." Sluggards want many things. They do not get them because they do not work for them. Diligent people often get what they want because they work hard.

In the Bible we find the word 'diligent' attached to important commands as well. God is concerned with His children's spiritual work ethic as well as what is accomplished. The word translated 'diligent' is the Greek word *spoudazo,* it has the basic meaning of earnest and eager exertion.

Diligence ensures success, when others consider quitting. To be a successful Christian Entrepreneur is to remain diligent in everything you do regardless of whether it is for the benefit of someone else or yourself. When you remain diligent, you will reap the benefits of your work.

God You Said....

- Do you see a man who excels in his work? He will stand before kings; He will not stand before unknown men. *(Proverbs 22:29)*

The destiny of the diligent is not the company of the obscure and insignificant.

God You Said....

- The hand of the diligent will rule, but the lazy man will be put to forced labor. *(Proverbs 12:24)*

Any Christian Entrepreneur who wants to have a position of authority and have his or her business bring glory to God, cannot dare to be lazy, wise people work hard, while fools waste time.

God You Said....

- The soul of a lazy man desires, and has nothing; but the soul of the diligent shall be made rich. *(Proverbs 13:4)*

Here the Christian Entrepreneur is told that hard work and diligence will produce both material gain and moral character.

God You Said....

- The lazy man does not roast what he took in hunting, but diligence is man's precious possession. *(Proverbs 12:27)*

Here the diligent makes wise use of their possessions and resources; the lazy waste them. Waste has become a way of life for many who live in a land of plenty. Waste is poor stewardship. Make good use of everything God has given you. The initial energy of hunting is nullified if one is too lazy to cook the game.

God You Said....

- And we desire that each one of you show the same diligence to the full assurance of hope until the end, that you do not become sluggish, but imitate those who through faith and patience inherit the promises. *(Hebrews 6:11-12)*

Hope keeps the Christian Entrepreneur from becoming lazy or feeling bored. Like an athlete, train hard and run well, remembering the reward that lies ahead. Faith looks to the One who promises; hope looks to the things promised. Philippians 3:14 says "I press toward the goal for the prize of the upward call of God in Christ Jesus."

God You Said....

- The lazy man says, "There is a lion outside! I shall be slain in the streets!" *(Proverbs 22:13)*

The Christian Entrepreneur has to recognize and realize that laziness invents bizarre excuses. The slothful man here talks of a lion outside, but considers not his real danger from the devil, that roaring lion within, and from his own slothfulness, which kills him.

God You Said....

- The plans of the diligent lead surely to plenty, but those of everyone who is hasty surely to poverty. *(Proverbs 21:5)*

Faithful completion of mundane tasks is a great accomplishment. Such work is patiently carried out according to a plan. Diligence does not come naturally to most people; it is a result of strong character. Don't look for quick and easy answers. Planning typically leads to plenty, and hast to poverty. It is not wrong to plan, but it is wrong to plan what the Lord has expressly forbidden.

God You Said....

- Go to the ant, you sluggard! Consider her ways and be wise, which, having no captain, overseer or ruler, provides her supplies in the summer, and gathers her food in the harvest. How long will you slumber, O sluggard? When will you rise from your sleep? A little sleep, a little slumber, a little folding of the hands to sleep-so shall your poverty come on you like a prowler, and your need like an armed man. *(Proverbs 6:6-11)*

The industrious insect's instinct shames lazy humanity! Proverbs condemns the sluggard's passivity, lack of initiative, the habit of procrastination, obliviousness to the dire results, and lack of discipline. This should not be so with the Christian Entrepreneur.

God You Said....

- Let him who stole steal no longer, but rather let him labor, working with his hands what is good, that he may have something to give him who has need. *(Ephesians 4:28)*

Note that the first motive for a Christian Entrepreneur to earn money is that he may have something to give. The occupational enterprise of the Christian Entrepreneur is not simply to make a living, but to make possible their being instruments of God's service to mankind through their work and giving.

God You Said....

- He who has a slack hand becomes poor, but the hand of the diligent makes rich. He who gathers in summer is a wise son; He who sleeps in harvest is a son who causes shame. *(Proverbs 10:4-5)*

Every day has 24 hours filled with opportunities to grow, serve, and be productive. Yet it is so easy to waste time, letting life slip from our grasp. Refuse to be a lazy person, sleeping or frittering away the hours meant for productive work. The Christian Entrepreneur should see time as God's gift and seize the opportunities to live and work diligently for Him.

God You Said....

• Prepare your outside work, make it fit for yourself in the field; and afterward build your house. *(Proverbs 24:27)*

The Christian Entrepreneur should first give attention to what is productive, then to what is comfortable.

God You Said....

• In all labor there is profit, but idle chatter leads only to poverty. *(Proverbs 14:23)*

The Christian Entrepreneur has to understand that in the battle of values, industrious work wins over mere talk. As you labor in your business everyday, you can expect to be profitable. The farmer goes out and plant seeds and expects a harvest. The Christian Entrepreneur who is planting seed after seed in their business and laboring in their business, again can expect to do well. God is not a man that He should lie, nor the son of man that He should repent. If He said it, He meant it.

God You Said....

• Do not love sleep, lest you come to poverty; Open your eyes, and you will be satisfied with bread. *(Proverbs 20:13)*

Sleep is a gift from God that restores a person's energy and vitality. Yet sleep can also be a matter of excess and laziness. Hard work is necessary in order to run a successful business and to make a living, laziness leads only to poverty.

God You Said....

• The lazy man will not plow because of winter; he will beg during harvest and have nothing. *(Proverbs 20:4)*

We have all heard similar warnings; if you don't study, you'll fail the test; if you don't save, you won't have money when you need it. If you don't prospect, you will not have any customers. God wants us to anticipate future needs and prepare for them. We can't expect Him to come to our rescue when we cause our own problems through lack of planning and action. He provides for us, but He also expects us to be responsible. Please note, because the sluggard does not plow his field on time, he has nothing to harvest.

God You Said....

- The desire of the lazy man kills him, for his hands refuse to labor. He covets greedily all day long, but the righteous gives and does not spare. *(Proverbs 21:25-26)*

Here the Christian Entrepreneur has to understand that the longing of the lazy man kills him; he is devoured by his own passions because he will not expend the energy to fulfill them. Because the lazy man will not work, he can only covet what others have. The righteous hardworking person has more than enough and need not spare in giving.

God You Said....

- The Lord will command the blessing on you in your storehouses and in all to which you set your hand, and He will bless you in the land which the Lord your God is giving you. *(Deuteronomy 28:8)*

God promises to bless the Christian Entrepreneur as long as they do their duty and are not idle.

God You Said....

- A man's stomach shall be satisfied from the fruit of his mouth; from the produce of his lips he shall be filled. Death and life are in the power of the tongue, and those who love it will eat its fruit. *(Proverbs 18:20-21)*

The mouth and hands are our most productive members; success or failure depends on their proper use. A person's life largely reflects the fruit of his tongue. To speak life is to speak God's perspective on an issue of life; to speak death is to declare life's negatives, to declare defeat, or complain constantly. The Christian Entrepreneur should be speaking life into their business each and every single day.

God You Said....

- I went by the field of the slothful, and by the vineyard of the man void of understanding; And, lo, it was all grown over with thorns, and nettles had covered the face thereof, and the stone wall thereof was broken down. Then I saw, and considered it well: I looked upon it, and received instruction. Yet a little sleep, a little slumber, a little folding of the hands to sleep; So shall thy poverty come as one that traveleth; and thy want as an armed man. *(Proverbs 24:30-34)*

Here the slothful man is too lazy to keep thorns and nettles out of his vineyard or to keep his stone wall repaired. His laziness is further exhibited in sleeping late when he should be working. Therefore, his poverty will come as one that traveleth; that is, a bandit or vagabond. Small surrenders lead to great disasters.

God You Said....

- Whatever your hands finds to do, do it with your might; for there is no work or device or knowledge or wisdom in the grave where you are going. *(Ecclesiastes 9:10)*

It is possible that the Apostle Paul had this verse in mind when he wrote, "And whatever you do, do it heartily, as to the Lord and not to men" (Colossians 3:23). This affirmation is not a denial of a personal future state after death. Yet in relation to this world, the possibilities of working and learning have ceased. If we plan to do anything to the glory of God in this world, we had better do it while we still have time. Jesus said in John 9:4 "I must work the works of Him who sent Me while it is day, the night is coming when no one can work."

God You Said....

- Keep your heart with all diligence, for out of it spring the issues of life. *(Proverbs 4:23)*

Our heart, our feelings of love and desire dictates to a great extent how we live because we always fine time to do what we enjoy. Solomon tells us to guard our heart above all else, making sure we concentrate on those desires that will keep us on the right path.

Make sure your affections push you in the right direction. Put boundaries on your desires; don't go after everything you see. Look straight ahead, keep your eyes fixed on your goal, and don't get sidetracked on detours that lead to disappointments and setbacks.

God You Said....

- Therefore, my beloved brethren, be steadfast immovable, always abounding in the work of the Lord, knowing that your labor is not in vain in the Lord. *(1 Corinthians 15:58)*

The Christian Entrepreneur is to be steadfast and immovable, meaning he or she must stand one's ground, they must remain firm, strong, unshaken, and confident in the faith, in view of the truth that their company will be raised up. They must not be shaken or agitated with the strife's, the temptations, and cares of life. The Christian Entrepreneur is always abounding in the work of the Lord. Always engaged in doing the will of God; in promoting His glory, and advancing His Kingdom, this means to engaged diligently, laboriously; excelling in what He has called you to do, and that's to run and operate a successful Christian/Faith Based Business.

God You Said....

- And in every work that he began in the service of the house of God, in the law and in the commandment to seek his God, he did it with all his heart. So he prospered. *(2 Chronicles 31:21)*

As clearly as any of the proverbs, the author of II Chronicles outlines in the simplest terms the recipe for success: Seek God with all your heart and you will prosper. In all that Hezekiah attempted in God's service, he was earnest and single in his aim and dependence, and was prospered accordingly. Whether we have few or many talents entrusted to us, may we thus seek to improve them, and encourage others to do the same. Whatever is undertaken by the Christian Entrepreneur with a sincere regard to the glory of God, will succeed to their own honor and comfort.

God You Said....

- So she gleaned in the field until evening, and beat out what she had gleaned, and it was about an ephah of barley. *(Ruth 2:17)*

For the Christian Entrepreneur, Ruth 2:17 encourages industry, that in all labor, even that of gleaning, there is profit. Ruth was pleased with what she gained by her own industry, and was careful to secure it. Let the Christian Entrepreneur thus take care that they do not lose those things which they have wrought. Be diligent in all that God has given you and called you to do.

God You Said....

- But also for this very reason, giving all diligence, add to your faith virtue, to virtue knowledge, to knowledge self-control, to self-control perseverance, to perseverance godliness, to godliness brotherly kindness, and to brotherly kindness love. For if these things are yours and abound, you will be neither barren nor unfruitful in the knowledge of our Lord Jesus Christ. *(2 Peter 1:5-8)*

The Christian Entrepreneur has to let moral excellence be the mark of their life. In addition, add knowing God, self-control, endurance, godliness, and love, which will help his or her life to be meaningful and productive as they grow in their business.

1. **All diligence** - the Christian Entrepreneur life is a working life, diligence meaning ardent application and industry.

2. **In your faith** - this the Christian Entrepreneur has; but "faith alone" was never considered sufficient for salvation by any of the New Testament writers.

3. **Virtue** - primarily means courage, a grace particularly needed in the hostile marketplace.

4. **Knowledge** - this a different word from the full knowledge mentioned above, a possession the Christian Entrepreneur already has; and it therefore refers to a faithful continuation of their studies.

5. **Self-control** - this comes from the Greek word: engkrateia], "meaning the ability to take a grip of one's self."

6. **Patience** - in the New Testament, this word carries the thought of endurance and steadfast continuity in faithful service.

7. **Godliness** - this is the quality of honoring one's duties to God, standing in this list even higher than duties to one's fellow man. This conforms with the Savior's great pronouncement that the first and greatest commandment is to love God, and the second is to love man (Mark 12:18-30). Important as the love to man assuredly is, it is secondary to the duty of loving God and obeying his commandments. **Brotherly kindness** - this is from [Greek: philadelphia], founded on the Greek term [philo], meaning the love of brothers.

8. **Love** - this love ([Greek: agape]) is the highest type of love; it is more inclusive than [Greek: philadelphia], and is the kind of love God has for sinful, unworthy men.

God You Said….
- Set your mind on things above, not on things on the earth. *(Colossians 3:2)*

The thought of Christ and heaven being above and the sinful things of earth being below is misleading when understood merely in the sense of altitude. "The things above" are rather the things of higher importance, more exalted principles, and spiritual rather than carnal.

Are You a Diligent Person?
(Take this self-evaluation and find out.)

Check List To Be Diligent: True or False

Do you:

___1. Have a clear and precise vision for what you want to achieve?

___2. Creatively persist through disappointments and failures?

___3. Work Smart?

___4. "Rightly" Plan?

___5. "Rightly" Perform?

___6. Work Expeditiously (with target dates)?

___7. Work Efficiently?

___8. Work Effectively (achieving effective results)?

___9. Produce an end result that reflects a quality outcome?

___10. Attain true Excellence?

___11. Risk failure for a worthy goal?

___12. Practice self-disciplined?

___13. Procrastinate?

___14. Stay focused?

___15. Start working right away?

I think I am/am not a diligent person because:

_____

Chapter 5

THE CHRISTIAN ENTREPRENEUR & GOAL SETTING

Some Christian Entrepreneurs are so rigid in their schedules that any little 'crisis' ruins their day. Sometimes they stick to their plans even when the only reason for doing so is to save face. But the Apostle Paul did not share this rigidity. On more than one occasion in his missionary travels, Paul planned to invade a region with the gospel but the Spirit of God prevented him (Acts 16:6-7). Herein is balance: although Paul planned, he was sensitive to the Lord altering his plans.

In Proverbs 6, the author rebukes the man who prepares for nothing, calling him a "sluggard". He implores the sluggard to observe the ant which "prepares her food in the summer, and gathers her provision in the harvest" (v. 8). According to the Scriptures, the wise person in business will establish objectives and prepare for the future.

But that is not all. The wise Christian Entrepreneur will recognize his finiteness and subject his plans to the Lord. In James 4, the author specifically addresses the one who sets his goals in concrete: "Come now, you who say, 'Today or tomorrow, we shall go to such and such a city, and spend a year there and engage in business and make a profit.' Yet you do not know what your life will be like tomorrow. You are just a vapor that appears for a little while and then vanishes away" (vv. 13-14).

James calls such rigidity arrogance (v. 16). But he does not say that we should not set goals. Rather, we should make plans, but submit them to the Lord: "Instead, you ought to say, 'If the Lord wills, we shall live and also do this or that'" (v. 15).

In reality, James 4:15 balances out both extremes. We should use our *minds* and set goals, but we must do so in *humility*, recognizing that God alone controls our destiny, but the Christian Entrepreneur who repeatedly fails to meet even his projected deadlines will soon be out of work.

Setting goals is serious business. We ought not to be so anxious about life that we make rigid plans which are beyond our capacity to keep, nor should we be so lazy as to make no plans at all. Rather, with all humility, let us submit our plans to the Lord, and work for His glory.

What is a Goal?
A goal is an aim or objective intended to guide action toward a desired end.

The Bible has little or nothing to say about goals, it speaks at length about wisdom. Wisdom is a special kind of knowledge that leads to "good" or "right" actions. Christian Entrepreneurs must base their goal setting methodology upon biblical teachings on wisdom.

Setting Goals Effectively
1. Positive Statement - express your goals positively.

2. Be Precise – include dates, time & amounts.

3. Set Priorities – give each goal a priority (this helps you to avoid feeling overwhelmed by too many goals.

4. Write goals down – to avoid confusion.

Why Set Goals?
1. When goals are set, things happen.

2. Goals make you feel good about yourself.

3. Goals provide attitude adjustments.

4. Goals establish self-discipline and motivation.

5. Goals give you direction and purpose.

6. Goals take you where you want to go.

7. Goals create good habits and patterns to follow.

8. A goal will eliminate others from controlling your life. Set a goal to discipline yourself. If you don't others will.

Goals Can Be Negative If?

1. They are too big.

2. They are out of your sphere of interest.

3. You believe luck is necessary to arrive at your destination.

4. You set your goal by comparing yourself with others; accomplishments.

5. You are doing it for someone else.

Reasons Most People Do Not Set Goals:

1. They are not sold on the benefits.

2. They feel it's safer not to.

3. They fear commitment, failure or success.

4. They have a poor attitude or focus.

5. They don't want to work.

Setting a Goal

1. Decide exactly what you want – be very specific.

2. Aim high – you should have "butterflies." Stretch your limits.

3. Create visuals. The subconscious mind accepts all information as fact and cannot distinguish between what is real and what is imagined and believed.

4. Pick someone to emulate.

5. Define where you are. Goals must be "Big" according to your ability.

6. Determine what you are capable of in a day, a week, a month and a year.

7. Write your goals in detail and talk about them with appropriate people.

8. Focus on your goal daily. If a goal is not focused on for three days, it's as if it never existed.

9. See goals as if they had already happened.

10. Keep your FOCUS (Follow One Course Until Successful).

11. Quitting is not an option.

12. Set another goal immediately upon reaching a goal.

Visualizing Your Goals

By visualizing your goal your subconscious mind will work for you, behind the scenes, to encourage the manifestation of situations which will ultimately enable your goals to come true. A process of achieving your goals through the application of positive mental images will empower you to create a reality from your desires.

The subconscious mind will believe your visualizations as being real. We can use this faculty to consciously select images which we give to our subconscious. Conversely, as we meditate on our affirmations, the subconscious mind will rise to our awareness images and sensations of our successes; this is a clear indication that the affirmation/image has been accepted by our subconscious mind.

Goals Must Be S.M.A.R.T.

- **Specific** – goals must be specific, include the 5 components – who what, where, when, and how.

- **Measurable** – goals must be able to be measured to determine success; i.e. completion date, increase sales by 10%.

- **Actionable** – goals must be written in such a way that you must take action to complete them. Goals should not be passive!

- **Realistic** – if you do not have a clear, realistic understanding of what you are trying to achieve; it is difficult to set effective and realistic goals.

- **Timely** – time frames and completion dates must be assigned to each goal; i.e. within 2 weeks, by December 15th.

God You Said....
- Write the vision and make it plain on tables, that he may run who reads it. For the vision is yet for an appointed time; but at the end it will speak, and it will not lie. Though it tarries, wait for it; because it will surely come, it will not tarry. *(Habakkuk 2:2-3)*

Learn to look for and eagerly expect God to answer you. Wait as long as necessary for His answer. Write down what God shows you so that when those things happen, they will serve as a testimony to His faithfulness.

God You Said....
- The heart of the prudent acquires knowledge, and the ear of the wise seeks knowledge. *(Proverbs 18:15)*

There are three basic principles for making sound decisions: (1) Get the facts before answering; (2) Be open to new ideas and (3) make sure you hear both sides of the story before judging. All three principles center around seeking additional information.

God You Said....

- If the ax is dull, and one does not sharpen the edge, then he must use more strength; but wisdom brings success. (***Habakkuk 10:10***)

The wise person gets the job done much more quickly and efficiently than the fool who is compared to a dull ax.

God You Said....

- For which of you, intending to build a tower, does not sit down first and count the cost, whether he has enough to finish it. (***Luke 14:28***)

When the Christian Entrepreneur does not count the cost or estimates it inaccurately, their business may be left half built and then abandoned because they did not count the cost of the commitment to do it.

God You Said....

- The preparations of the heart belong to man, but the answer of the tongue is from the Lord. All the ways of a man are pure in his own eyes, but the Lord weighs the spirits. Commit your works to the Lord, and your thoughts will be established. (***Proverbs 16:1-3***)

If the Christian Entrepreneur turns over to the Lord what he plans to do, his life purposes will come to fruition.

God You Said....

- A man's heart plans his way, but the Lord directs his steps. (***Proverbs 16:9***)

The execution of the heart's plans is under God's control. The final outcome of the plans the Christian Entrepreneur makes is in God's hands. If this is so, why make plans? In doing God's will, there must be a partnership between the Christian Entrepreneur's

At such times, the only saving grace will be if the patient or dying elderly parent had given specific end of life care instructions to those in the family that walked closely with them through their illness or aging process to avoid unnecessary arguments or divided views. The bargaining person may also be the one dealing with a personal health crisis or is facing consequences with the laws for past misdoings or criminal activities. They may be bargaining with God that if he bails them out of the situation they will shape up and stop their bad habits.

The type of bargaining a person does is often a clue to areas of that person where guilt or unfinished business exists. It may be a quarrel or a misunderstanding that has remained unresolved for many reasons, including lack of inability to forgive from either party. Bargaining could also be someone telling God of all the better things and choices one would do or make if their families were restored or given a chance after a break-up. Even after my separation, I kept praying and hoping that some sudden miracle would bring me and my ex-husband back together, even though he continued harassing me even from a distance. I continued analyzing what I would change and invite him to change and passionately offered these thoughts to God in prayer. An example was for me to be honest and outspoken with my likes and dislikes as things that had continuously hurt me yet for the sake of peace I rarely told him for fear of his anger, but instead I kept piling them up in my heart to a point of unredeemable damage. This went on until he asked for divorce as a final blow to my continued hopes for reconciliation. Like many others in my circumstances, I lived in denial always hoping against hope.

In our intervention, we must realize that in this stage those battling with grief may intentionally keep themselves very busy to avoid or delay facing or dealing with their grief and the pain of their loss as they should. Those helping them must be willing to listen even to the unspoken pain and be attentive to any thing they might do after this to hurt themselves on realizing that it is too late to achieve their bargains. Caringly explain to them that their feelings of guilt and wishful thinking are a normal and genuine part of the grieving process. If on the other hand their grief is justified, help them get to a point of forgiving themselves and others in order to be able to move on. It may be necessary to refer them to their spiritual leaders for further guidance and nurturing.

4. <u>Depression.</u>

Depending on what is causing depression in one's life, reality will gradually hit home. It may be expected in the case of a major terminal illness where the patient has gradually declined to a point of total helplessness and poor quality of life for several years or months. Some may even have been in a hospital, a nursing home etc. Changes may have happened in their health clearly indicating that their vital organs were slowly shutting up and they may even be on a ventilator. They may also have started refusing food or medicine and constantly saying that they are "ready to go home". Some may suddenly withdraw and ask to be left alone or even become hostile and unpleasant. They may also appear depressed and praying for God to take them out of their misery. Those with spouses, children or elderly parents dependent on them may be torn apart with moments of wanting to get well and back in circulation with their loved ones while at other moments they feel too sick and wanting out of their situation. They may be anxious and worried about the fate of their loved ones when they die. All these situations often lead to feelings of depression and great anxiety where the grieving person does not know what to ask for from God. They may go through episodes of agitation, deep sadness, sleeplessness, and many episodes of unexplained crying. While all this is going on with the sick or dying one, the family or caregivers may start picking up clues of real decline and imminent death soon. These may quickly trigger up all kinds of depressive reactions from different people and the whole atmosphere may become very volatile and charged with fear, uncertainty and anticipatory grief. The pain of having to let go of the dying loved one and the thought of a future life without them must be painful and depressive. Some caregivers and family members, who have concentrated all their time and focus in the care of this person, might start panicking as to what they will do when death eventually carries their loved one away. There may be a deep sense of emptiness and meaningless life in the anticipation of the sick person's absence. The fear of the unknown future without one's long time spouse, parent or one's child may linger on for months after they are long gone. All these can quickly result in serious depression if care and intervention are not given.

One way of intervening is helping the grieving person to see that their feelings are normal in their journey with grief and that you are willing to walk with them until they feel more comfortable with their situation. Let them know also that they may be in and out of this for unspecified periods until depression gradually fades away. Depression may also be a positive reaction in the healing process as it allows the grieving person to experience their pain and loss realistically and truthfully.

In some cases, depression may be so severe, affecting the grieving person, family and friends and isolating them to the extent that medical intervention may become necessary. Emotional support, empathy and education are all very helpful and significant elements of healing recovery of the grieving person(s).

5. <u>Accepting:</u>

Inevitably, the mourner begins to face the hard reality emotionally and intellectually that their loved one is indeed gone and is no longer physically present in this life. In other cases the grieving person realizes that they are really divorced and each person must now face life alone after many years of married

31

life. Others suddenly face the permanence of their paralysis, amputation or blindness, where they can no longer do all the things they automatically and easily did and took for granted in the past like all of us.

Accepting does not in any way indicate that we like what has happened to us or the losses we have encountered. It just means we have accepted the reality of our loss and grief and will try to find ways and means or redirecting our energy to our future gradually, instead of permanently focusing on the past. It is a step of reconciling ourselves with the reality and finding a way to cope and move on with life as best as may be humanly possible. This is the time the grieving person faces the need to adapt to the new environment. There will be new challenges of being a single parent again, rethinking and reorganizing the parenting styles to adapt to your new life. There may be the initial resentment of these new roles so suddenly imposed on the grieving person by each individual circumstances, while at the same time realizing that the best one can do is reconcile with the situation and move on with life as best as possible.

When the grieving person accepts and reconciles themselves to the new roles and responsibilities, they will feel better and more comfortable with their healing process. There will still be days which are harder than others, but the best one can do is take one step one day at a time. After the worst emotional storm that took all their energies is over, it will be possible to see some light at the end of the tunnel and feel some sense of hope for better days ahead. It will be wise at that point to reinvest their emotional energy into new assignments, hobbies, new friendships and other activities that will begin to shape the new person in a new horizon of life. It will get better and more comfortable to start navigating one's life into new directions, making future plans without the guilt of abandoning the memories of their departed loved one or even their past lives. At this point, the grieving person will be more confident in looking at new and different opportunities in life with a sense and desire of healing oneself and those dependent on them.

Our faith and trust in a God who can strengthen us for each small step or day, carry us through our challenges when we can barely walk. The words of "The Footprints" may be our best help through such crossroads of life. It may literary be a journey of "one little step at a time". It may at times feel like one is taking two steps forward and one step backward resulting in a very slow healing process, until we are strong enough and feeling confident about our process. This season of grief and bereavement varies from person to person based on many reasons and what loss one is grieving. There is not a firm set of rules on how to go through all this but it depends on individuals.

This stage may also facilitate the healing process, developing of a new environment of personal growth, new relationships and activities. It also brings a new hope for better and manageable days ahead. As we learn to accept our losses of one kind or another, we are able to seek new directions in life while remembering our past loses with less pain. Sifting through our memories to see what we can carry from our past to enrich our future and what needs to be discarded for ever to avoid being shackled by the pain of our past for ever. This gradually empowers and encourages us to seek new opportunities to help us continue with our dreams little by little, at times even sustaining the legacies of our loved ones now gone before us. We learn to live with their good memories that might even become support pillars and strengths for us in the future. One can never quite forget the pain of losing, but one gradually begins to accept the fact that perhaps it was good that our loved ones were healed in a different way, never to suffer any more. We can gradually acknowledge these feelings without guilt.

In our intervention, we need to reassure the grieving person that grief is very personal and they must allow themselves to go through it at their own comfortable and manageable pace. Help them understand too that accepting the death of a loved one and getting reconciled with this or other losses in life is not to be viewed as forgetting them or pretending that whatever else we lost in life did not hurt us. Accepting and beginning to look forward into the future, even after a divorce, loss of important limbs like arms and legs, loss of our sight or any major disability is actually a good sign that the journey of healing is finally beginning. Inevitably, there will be many obstacles along the way, but with God on our side and with the help of friends, families and other professionals and support systems availed to us, and we will gradually begin to see some light of hope and healing at the end of our tunnel of grief and loss. However, every grieving person must be patient with themselves and others in this process which is a life changing journey. Like David, (Psalm 121 verses 1, 3 & 8) we will do well to "Look up unto the mountains, does my help come from there?", "He will not let you stumble and fall; the one who watches over you will not sleep". Remembering too that, "The Lord keeps watch over you as you come and go, both now and for ever ". I would want nothing more than the assurance that God will be there for me at all times, even when I am too broken to pray or do anything for myself because "His plans for my life are good, they are good and not for disaster, to give me a future and a hope" Jeremiah 29 verse 11 (KJ Version).

a) Physical Symptoms

There all kinds of physical manifestations of grief and bereavement including too little or too much sleep, loss of appetite, fatigue, unexplained pains and aches everywhere, etc. Unless these issues are adequately and promptly dealt with, there is a likelihood of them resulting in long term problems long after the grieving period. They could very easily change the grieving person's lifestyle from being healthy and active to being withdrawn, dull and sedentary in an unhealthy way.

b) Emotional Symptoms

These symptoms include panic attacks, depression, sadness, numbness, disbelief, hostility, anger, loneliness, emptiness, shock, decreased self-esteem, jealousy, disorientation, helplessness, hopelessness, self-hate, feelings of rejection, withdrawal from others, confusion etc. Grief is wanting and loving those that are dear and precious to our hearts and lives, never wanting to let go of them. After a long illness, there may be relief for self and deceased, often accompanied by a sense of guilt for such feelings. All this is normal and natural part of grieving. There will also be moments of inability to concentrate and focus as we reflect on the absence of the touch and voice of our beloved now gone beyond the grave.

c) Spiritual Symptoms

Regardless of whether the grieving person is a believer or not, the initial shock and impact of grief will often trigger anger against God for allowing the death while we have been praying and trusting Him for healing. At the same time, the spirit will be deeply and passionately seeking God's comfort, consolation, encouragement and help to survive the loss to death. It is wise to allow ourselves and those we may be trying to comfort, console and support to express their feelings in order to clear their minds, empty themselves of the anger and thus be able to look up to God as a helper and not an enemy in the tragedy. Participation of the grieving persons, however young or old, in the funeral arrangements and other rituals will help them to come to terms with the reality of their loss. This will also help them come to some form of closure and move towards some new meaning to life without the deceased loved one.

d) Behavioral Symptoms

During the initial shock of grief and bereavement, some people will deal with it by avoiding and blocking the memories and reality of the situation for a while. Some will cry ceaselessly while others will become motionless and void of emotions. Even these are normal and natural reactions that must not be ridiculed or viewed as stupid. It is important to honor and acknowledge our own or other people's individuality in moments of intense grief and bereavement and allow each person to process their grief in whichever way they feel comfortable. These are the same reasons why we see many behavioral variations of highs and lows of grief during major holidays and anniversaries.

It also helps to remind the grieving person that *"Jesus wept"* (John 11:35) He was grieving the death of his close friend Lazarus. He gave us permission to express our sorrow and pain in tears. Isaiah also refers to Jesus in Isaiah 53:3 as *"A man of sorrows Acquainted with bitterest grief"*. We can therefore trust Jesus to understand our heartaches and grief because he has his own first hand experience. God our father_understands too, having experienced a grief too deep and painful that He looked the other way when his son was dying on the cross at Calvary covered with all the sins of humanity.

In general, there is no set timetable for grief. The depth and impact of grief depends on the kind of relationship that existed with the deceased loved one. There is a common saying that "Time heals all the wounds". For some it does but for some it does not and there is no telling how long the pain and intensity of their loss will linger on. All we can do is hang in there until the situation slows down and becomes manageable. It is therefore very important to wait before making any major decisions while the mind is still confused and cannot focus realistically or rationally.

5

ANTICIPATORY GRIEF FOR THE
TERMINALLY ILL AND THEIR CAREGIVERS

When a patient receives the diagnosis of a terminal illness like cancer of any kind, major debilitating heart ailments and many others, the shocking news often sends messages of a death sentence; images of a life soon coming to an end however long or short the illness may take before death finally strikes. I cannot even try to imagine the kind of painful thoughts that must run through the minds of the patient at that instance and from then on.

There may be anger at the possibility of not being able to live long enough to achieve one's dreams and aspirations like everyone else in life. I am thinking of a parent who has so many plans for the growing family. Dependent on the age of the children, there must be wonderings and panic attacks as to what will happen to their young children once they die. Terminal illnesses have been known to strike suddenly into the life of an engaged couple with well advanced wedding arrangements with a hope for a bright and long future in marriage together. Suddenly there is need to continue with the arrangements knowing that they may only be together in their marriage for a brief moment before one takes over the compounded role of a caregiver/spouse. Many of the original plans about their future must then be altered in many ways to help cope with the terminal diagnosis.

Anticipatory grief may strike into the life a young and excited person newly graduated, lots of plans and expectations for a bright professional life ahead with the sky as the only limit. The impact of such news must inevitably be devastating after many years of hard work and sacrifices to achieve their academic heights only to realize they might not live long enough to enjoy the fruits of their labors or even make the differences they anticipated albeit in a little way for their families or communities. At the prime of their age, many people at this stage in life have found such news and the anticipatory grief too much to bear and have quickly taken their lives or gone into total depression, helplessness and hopelessness (dependent on their diagnosis, especially the irreversible/incurable HIV/ AIDS) resulting in suicides in many cases.

Anticipatory grief for any family or individual can be so debilitating that it almost halts everyone's life, current or future plans both in private or public life. The fear of not knowing what the impact and progression of the illness will be like may be the hardest thing for the patient and the caregiver to contend with. The impact that complicates the grief may vary from finances, how slow or fast the health will decline, what complications may arise, the management of the patient's care and the needs of the other affected family members. It may be that the terminally ill patient is an adult child who has been caring for elderly parents.

These parents must be drastically affected and threatened by such news and begin to grieve a future without their child/ caregiver. The child/caregiver must also begin to grieve the pain of perhaps dying earlier and leaving helpless parents behind.

For both the terminally ill and the caregiver, the challenge is to shift and change their past lifestyle to accommodate the new needs for care, be able to focus on and act differently on the emotional, behavioral, psychological and spiritual mindsets that may now appear as this journey continues. The past and current interpersonal relationships between everyone in this circle will be major determining factors as to how they live and relate for the remaining part of their life together. The life and future of everyone involved will change one way or the other. The initial period may be turbulent and feel like they are thrown into a whirlpool of activities and changes, not knowing how things will be like when things finally fall into place. This is when the presence of a higher power like God for believers becomes a paramount necessity to bring some kind of meaning and normalcy to the life ahead and maintain some stability to continue. Support from friends and family will also go a long way under these circumstances. Everyone involved will get to a point of accepting the reality that this diagnosis is not changing and that sooner this terminally ill person will be gone for good. Along the way, changes must be made to care for them and take over some of the responsibilities they handled for themselves and their families. Those remaining behind must now face the reality of life ahead minus the sick spouse, parent, child or even a close/best friend and confidante. This may be the toughest stage in this journey because people walk their grief and part of the morning along the way even before death takes their loved one away. However, some people go through it in denial, hoping against hope that the sick person will heal and life will continue as normal as always. Everyone in this circle may get into some frantic activities trying to make the best use of the remaining time, make it up to each other or even make necessary plans for the future of the ailing patient and the survivors thereafter. The issue of acceptance and facing the reality of this matter determines a great deal what happens in everyone's future. In some cases, prayerfully and with support from everyone involved, both parties are able to walk through this "valley of the shadow of death" (Psalm 23:4) and will in some cases start doing "their good-byes", exchange forgiveness and blessings towards each other and even develop greater yearnings for whatever would pave a way for them to meet and live together in eternity after the separation that death brings. Many hard headed people who ignored salvation and the need for God have been known to suddenly call for and seek God when everything they thought invaluable now appears truly perishable and temporal as we all are. Dealing with anticipatory grief does not mean one will not grieve after the death of the terminally ill patient. Anticipatory grief may even trigger or revive past grief or bereavement that was not adequately dealt with and brought to some kind of closure. Some people grieve in the open while others do it in private and don't even want anyone to ask or talk about it with them. Tradition, culture and age may also dictate how we express our grief and bereavement.

When the terminally patient finally dies, there will still be the initial shock and finality of a journey through the illness. The intensity of the grief will be dependent on many dynamics like the relationships that existed, whether there are any unfinished businesses or grudges and the support around for the survivors and the caregivers whose lives might feel empty and meaningless for a while until they pick up their own lives gradually and continue as best as they can. The intensity of the grief will gradually decrease but should not be measured or compared with anyone else. One gradually finds a time and place to laugh, joke, cry, or just have fun somewhere along the future. These should be viewed as normal and necessary points of the healing process and no one should be condemned for such feelings. They are actually necessary signs and symptoms of acceptance of the situation and that gradual healing is taking place. Do not hurry the process, but be ready to walk this path one step at a time. Days will be different and so will be the moods.

Mr. Stephen Levine cautions us that *"Unattended sorrow narrows the paths of our lives"* It will therefore be a hindrance to our healing and progress in the future. Un-acknowledged grief may eventually be our worst enemy into the future.

We must therefore allow ourselves to feel our grief, be it anticipatory, current or in the future. Only the grieving or bereaved person knows the real implications and depth of their loss and they should be allowed to deal with their bereavement individually. No two people will grieve or mourn in the same manner even in the case of two parents who are both struggling with the loss of their child. Neither will two siblings go through the same emotions at the loss of a common parent. Different genders, age groups, social groupings, cultural backgrounds affect how different people deal with their losses. No one should be made to feel ashamed of their tears or brokenness at moments of grief and loss. At any rate these are necessary responses in the days, months, years and life ahead as the affected persons work towards some form of normalcy in their shattered lives thereafter. Complicated grief may also result from the death of a parent, sibling or ex-spouse with whom we should have had better relationship. Our dreams and hopes of reconciling for a happy ending may surface and disturb us. At the time some people feel like the deceased "haunts you from the grave". We must find a way of completing this grief. In order to move on with life, complete our unmet hopes and dreams and expectations that were not previously achieved. It may take experiencing the unfinished events in order to tell them what you would have said, if you had been given a chance or had known how to do that. "There is sacredness in tears. They are not a mark of weakness but of power. They speak more eloquently than 10,000 tongues. They are the messengers of overwhelming grief, of deep contrition and unspeakable love". (Washington Irving.)

41

Kept on the inside, tears turn into more bottled heartache and ceaseless pain. Allowed to flow freely, they are cleansing, relieving and healing to the soul. Tears are as old as God's creation and neither could Jesus resist the need to weep when he received the news of the death of his great friend Lazarus from his sisters Martha and Mary. (John 11:35). Jesus therefore knows fully the pain of grief and loss

6

Major Depression and Complicated Grief

This is also known as unresolved grief. After the loss of a loved one, it is common for people to experience a deep sense of sadness, bouts of crying, anger, pain and even depression. Unless one is careful and surrounded by caring and understanding family and friends, about 1 in 5 bereaved people will develop major depression. However, depression can be handled with medicine, counseling or other forms of therapy of one's choice. But it is very important that something is done about it before it is too late and the grieving person becomes suicidal or self-destructive. Some symptoms of complicated grief are:

- continued disbelief in the death of the loved one

- inability to accept the death

- flash-backs, nightmares, memories that keep intruding into thoughts over time

- severe prolonged grief symptoms: anger, sadness or depression

- keeping a fantasy relationship with the deceased with feelings that he/she is always present, watching or haunting
- continuous yearning and searching for the deceased
- unusual symptoms that seem unrelated to the death (physical symptoms, strange or abnormal behavior)
- breaking off ties to social contact and withdrawing from everything

In cases of divorce and separation, your "less loved one" may still be alive. You will need to find ways of healing your past pain, even when your ex-spouse will not change. You must look beyond the loss and be intentional about moving on with life before things get too complicated to handle. You will bring better value and meaning into your own life, removing the shackles and limitations of painful reminders of a relationship that never lived up to your expectations. Regardless of whether one's grief emanates from the death of a loved one or other painful experiences in life like divorce and separation, here are some symptoms of major depression that cannot be explained by normal bereavement:

- constant thoughts of being worthless or hopeless
- ongoing thoughts of death or suicide (other than thoughts that they would be better dead or should have died with their loved one)
- being unable to perform day-to-day activities
- guilt over things done or not done at the time of the loved one's death
- delusions (beliefs that are not true)

- hallucinations (hearing voices or seeing things that are not there) except for "visions" in which the person briefly hears or sees the deceased
- slower body responses and reactions
- extreme weight loss or gain
- symptoms lasting more than 2 months after the loss

Considering that the intense grief and loss alone is enough to negatively impact anyone's health, it is important that anyone experiencing any of the above symptoms consults or seeks help from qualified health or mental health professionals. Proper treatment is imperative because people dealing with complicated or unresolved grief have a much higher risk of an emotional mental breakdown or becoming worse and suicidal. Life might even seem to have come to a standstill for the grieving person and they will need someone to shake them from the daze.

7

DIFFERENT KINDS OF LOSSES

Feelings of loss are very personal and the only person who can fully describe their significance is the one who is personally experiencing or undergoing them. As mentioned earlier, there are many losses and challenges as we travel through life that result in grief, other than just the death of a loved one, be it a family or friend. Again, the extent of the grief each will cause is dependent on the value of what is lost and the implications of its loss and absence from our lives. Such losses will include:

Death of a parent/child	Death of a spouse	Death of a partner
Death of a roommate	Death of a sibling	Death of a close friend
Death of a relative	Death of a colleague	Death of a classmate
Death of a pet	Serious illness of a loved one	Broken Relationships
Loss of innocence in rape etc.	Loss of health through illness	Loss of mental ability
Loss of financial security	Leaving Home	Change of a job
Loss of physical ability	Graduation from school	Loss of a home

Unfortunately, as humanity advances in civilization and technological knowledge, there will be increased new losses to be grieved by each of us. Traditions and cultures of the world continue to change in many ways. Some have proved worth and necessary doing away with. But the loss of some of our traditions and cultures have seriously depleted and minimized our family support systems to the extent that many children and elderly members are lonely and helpless because the aspect of the extended families is less and less. I can only imagine the grief of those who grew up in such surroundings, those who knew the positive impact of extended families, but now have to fend for themselves in their own old age. I will however, highlight just a few of the above mentioned losses and the grief they bring to people's lives today.

GRIEVING THE DEATH OF A CHILD:

When you lose a child you lose your future.

Compassionate Friends say the loss of one's child, our future and hope, is the worst anyone should ever have to endure. It exposes one to deep spiritual battles and questions, deep anger at God and life, including those around us. It brings guilt that our genetic compositions might have endangered our child whether born prematurely, dead or whether they die later. A child's death may also trigger the guilt of not caring for one's child properly and protecting them from all harm in some unfortunate circumstances. One may also feel guilt that our choices and family lifestyles killed our children and the ensuing grief may be unbearable. Others conclude that perhaps God punished our wrong doings by killing our children.

The most painful reality is that even though it happens often, no parents have ever expected to bury their children and then continue living after that. It should be the other way around. Guilt and grief may also result from the fact that the parent old and far gone in life, is still alive instead of a child who dies too early even before their lives "begin". These feelings of grief will still arise, even when a child has been terminally ill right from their birth and they were never expected to live long. There is always a feeling of hoping against hope that this child will somehow outlive the parent. It happens many times over, that after the death of one's child young or as an adult, parents have been known to lose interest in life, start declining and die soon after that. In an Emergency Room incident, when a little 2 year old boy was rushed in with a full arrest only to lose his battle to a heart disease, I heard a heart broken father say in the midst of his painful sobbing *"Something died in me when my son stopped breathing and I don't know if I will ever recover from this loss"*. We were informed later that this little toddler had already undergone two heart surgeries and was scheduled to go through a third one in two weeks time. But even though all along the parents and the large family that came had known he was critically ill, it was still an unbearable loss that crashed all those of us present in the ER that fateful morning. Many have been heard to say that life has lost its meaning after such a loss. I know this for a fact, having watched my own mother completely lose herself when my brother (2nd born in a family of 10 children) died instantly in a motor vehicle accident. Even though my mother lived for another 12 years after that, she was never the same and would speak about him constantly. Grief took a great toll on her and my father after the death of yet another of my younger brother as a result of a liver problem. My father quickly went down with his grief and my mother who was his immediate caregiver with our back-up succumbed to grief four months after my father's death. Both of them were very open and frank with me that their children's deaths were the worst that could happen to them. My mother openly told me one day in a conversation that she did not want to live long enough to have to burry any one else after that. Within three weeks of saying this to me, my mother passed away.

49

Sudden or unexpected death comes with great denial and disbelief as in a motor vehicle accident. There is trauma and shattered dreams for the diseased child. If a child dies in a homicide or accident, there will be various complications in the grieving process for the family and friends. The involvement of a coroner and other legal implications, going to the courts, listening to and giving testimonies, further prolongs and complicates the grieving process for the family and everyone else involved in the loss.

The grieving parent may be left deeply angry that the person who killed their child is still alive and might still have a second chance to life after serving their prison sentence while their child's life is brutally terminated for ever. This may also result in anger against God for not protecting their child from this sudden death. In some very sad situations, especially where family relations were already tense and not agreeable, such a sudden death could turn into a vicious cycle with different family members blaming each other for not being there. Many marriages have been known to break down with this as the last straw.

It is not unusual to find a grieving parent commit suicide or do some drastic things either to self or others as they struggle with the anger and guilt of being alive while their child who deserved to live is dead. Mothers have been known to reject other surviving children, even refusing to nurse babies in their torment of loss and grief. It is at this time that pastoral care givers and everyone around such grief need to be extremely careful not to rationalize the situation. At times it is best just be a silent support and presence until the intensity of their grief subsides and they can start dealing with it better. In our anxiety to say something, we may end up doing greater damage than help. Great patience and compassion will be needed.

Long term illness in children has a very deep effect as they journey through some very turbulent and intense places of pain, confusion and helplessness. It is equally devastating for any parent or guardian to watch them helplessly suffer in and out of the hospital yet knowing there is nothing you can do to change the situation other than encourage, remain present and make them as comfortable as possible. This is even harder in the case of a child who is born with a life threatening condition that will be their journeying companions till death. During this period, if there are other children in the family, they may feel left out as all the attention is on the sick one until they finally pass away.

When this child finally dies, the family might be torn between feeling a sense of relief that this child is at rest and not suffering any more. But guilty feelings may also creep into their lives wondering if there is anything they might have done differently in their care. But gradually, as the situation gets better, the parents and others in the family might benefit from getting involved into a support group of other parents who have gone through such an experience or loss. But we do need to constantly remember that grief is very personal and how we grieve will very much depend on the personal relationships we had with our departed loved one.

Grieving the Loss of a Spouse:

When you lose your spouse, you lose your present.

The death of a spouse is an earth shattering blow that brings incomprehensible pain. This often means the loss of your best friend and the most intimate relationship, bridge partner, companion and your hope for the future. This means the end of that passionate goodnight kiss, the straightening of a tie as you leave home for work or for a meeting or a reassuring pat on the shoulder. When a life partner dies, your identity dies with them. You are soon given a new identity as a "widow or a widower". These become labels that communicate a very harsh reality, and some unbearable sadness. Yet in many cases the people around widows and widowers are not even aware of this fact.

Discovering who you are after a death of a spouse

The loss of a spouse to death quickly moves the surviving spouse from the category of "married" to "widowed. As in all other loses, it is a transition in life without preparation and often times with no fore-warning. It challenges the widowed to restructure their lives following this enormous change. It sets you on a path to redefine yourself and create a whole new landscape or new uncharted territory for your future. It is a defining moment for who you will become. Newly widowed, one is called to blaze a new trail for their lives from this point forth. You will need to renegotiate everything as one who will be living on your own, with decreased options.

The death of a spouse tears through every layer of one's existence.

Losing a spouse is most often losing one's best friend. Some of the physical manifestations of the impact of your grief may include – ulcers, colitis, rheumatoid arthritis, rapid heartbeat, high blood pressure, back pain, dizziness, etc. Your immune system may also be compromised resulting in intermittent colds and other minor illnesses. Anger at God, at the loved one who died, your family and everything else may also be part of your grieving process. This too is normal. Be honest with God about it as you pray for help because He knows and understands exactly what you are going through, even when those around you want to but cannot fully appreciate the depth of your loss. (Psalm 22:1-2, 19)

The scars from your grief and the healing process from your loss will ALWAYS be a part of your life from this time forth. It will be part of your new identity. However grief does not have to be the defining factor for the quality of the rest of your life. It is okay to live, learn and gradually to love again as time goes by. You can incorporate your loss and use it to forge a new identity that helps you continue growing. Your faith traditions can also help giving meaning to loss, and the hope of an eternal connection to your loved one. As you choose to ritually mark your grief during important anniversaries and holidays, it will allow for a softening of the repeated reminders of your loss.

Learn new skills, meet new people, take up new hobbies and intentionally strive to live on as best as God helps you. Perhaps this is what your departed spouse would actually want you to do. To continue the dreams and projects you started and enjoyed together.

It will be necessary to learn to live with and accommodate your loss and make it a part of who you are. It is a part of your new identity that needs to be embraced and accepted. It may be tough at the beginning but necessary for your healing. Good self care will include eating balanced and nutritious meals; enough rest, regular exercise, taking some necessary vitamins, etc. Get your regular medical checkups, especially if you had been putting them off as you focused all your time, resources and energy on the care for your loved one.

You are not alone in your widowhood. However, acknowledge the uniqueness of your personal situation. The uniqueness of your sorrow may come from

>Length of your marriage
>The age of your spouse
>Circumstances of death
>Your gender and age
>Your family's coping mechanism & communication style
>Cultural & religious orientation
>Financial, social issues
>Children or no children

Embrace your situation. Honor it. Affirm its reality. While grief is devastating, it is also fertile ground for some mystical experiences. Only then will you be able to pick up the broken pieces of your life and move on.

Acknowledge the many losses caused by the death of your spouse in order to refocus and make NEW BEGINNINGS.

Not only is this a physical loss of your spouse, but also:

The loss of your high school sweet heart
Your first love
Your best friend and confidante
Your lover & soul-mate
Your dance partner & traveling companion
Your chef, your gardener, your chauffeur, your accountant
Your comedian, encourager, pillar of strength,
And many other roles they played in your life.

Being single again, no matter how long or short you have been married is DIFFERENT. But you do not become any less important, nor should you allow others to make you feel that way for any reason. Loneliness is something nobody wants to experience, but it will be inevitable at the beginning. But the Lord promises to stay with you and help you through your grief. He will not abandon you. (Psalm 139:1-17), (John 14:18-19). He will watch your going out and your coming back, both now and for ever. (Psalm 121:8)

Rediscovering Purpose & Meaning in Life:

The measure of your grief is the measure of how much you loved your dearly departed spouse. While their absence hurts as deeply as you loved them, I'd rather that was my experience rather than the painful regrets from unfulfilled life and dreams.

Our grieving is part of life, not something removed from it. It is gradually transformed into something closer to remembering and cherishing with gratitude, a warm comforting glow instead of a hot burning fire. As you go deeper into your pain, you encounter persons, events, words, elements of creation that bring small nuggets and graces of healing. Trust this sacred rhythm; open yourself to these occasions of grace. They are gracious gifts, gracious assistance for your journey through grief. As you go through these "soul breaking" moments, your deep contemplation of the beautiful relations you had with your beloved, will be the most creative human response to the "shredding of your soul by the grief you feel. Soothe your aching heart with the richness of your memories.

You might want to set a small memorial space in a private corner of your house with a picture of your loved one and some tokens that recall and signify your special relationship. You have not lost the memories that you spun together, nor the impact that your beloved had on your life, the values you learnt from them and the interests you both developed and shared over the years. Watching family videos and family pictures from the past become important and helpful ways to bring back into remembrance some good old days. Some of the memories may be painful reminders at the beginning, but they will one day be precious treasures you will be glad to have. Creating a family heirloom from the relationship you had with your dearly departed will not only be good for your current family members and friends who share your loss today, but also for future generations.

To give healthy and helpful meaning to your new life and New Beginnings, it will help to intentionally give meaning to the life and death of your loved one. The journey will at times take you through some very bumpy places and phases. These may include moments of intense anger, deep sorrow, terrifying fear, etc. The path to the new horizons of your new different life may cause you to feel like a passenger on a long and at times uncomfortable journey that you did not sign up for, but were booked on nonetheless.

In search of meaning and purpose to life, embrace the importance of your faith and spirituality. In an effort to survive and find the necessary support, it may be time to join a regular church family if you do not have one already.

New beginnings encourage you to re-discover a reason to get your feet out of bed, even when you really don't feel like doing so. It propels you to gradually step out of your sorrow, even out of your home, after your life line, your spouse has been terminally and permanently severed. You are encouraged to step out into the track of life and living, praying and trusting God for grace enough for every new day. Just as He promised Joshua of olden days, He will never forsake or leave you alone. Not now, not ever. He will keep you in perfect peace if you can trust him with your future and fix your thoughts on him even for what you think is impossible. (Isaiah 26: 3)

Re-evaluating and Refocusing on Life:

Be aware that the death of a spouse may trigger thoughts of your own eventual death, either because this is a reality for each of us, or because perhaps you too are sick etc.

Give your grief the necessary space and time which differs from person to person. If you stay too busy to grieve, eventually the body will find a way of grounding you from running away. Find a way of balancing between going overboard with too many activities to total resignation and giving up on life for good. Your spirit too is grieving and you might be going through a "dark night of the soul". Remember that a loving God will stand with you in your loss and grief. Those who care about you cannot grieve for you, but they can and are willing to light up the candles to help you find your way through the dark night if you reach out to them. Help them to help you by being honest with them. Don't always say "I'm fine". Let some people know how terribly you actually feel at times. Your grief is real and you should not sugar coat, down play or hide it.

You may not ever get over your grief, but with God's help and the support of family friends and support group, you gradually go through it. The truth is that there is no way over, under or around grief. As you allow yourself to experience grief without "fight or flight' you will notice a gradual change for better. You may be alone on this

ride but never completely as a helpless victim, regardless of how your loved one might have died.

Take heart. While the wound of grief is so painful and we naturally wish it would pass faster than it does, it is a season in which we learn lessons that would not have been possible if we had short-circuited the grieving process. We experience and learn of the incredible resilience of the human spirit. We also find out that if we give grief its dues, sorrow returns the favor by giving us a precious gift – the assurance that we have indeed loved deeply in this lifetime. This is by far the greatest achievement in life. Allow yourself to feel good when those moments come. Happiness is never a betrayal of your love for your departed spouse.

As often as you can, remind yourself of your reasons for living on. You have a future worth enduring for, and you have the right and the reason to feel a renewed sense of purpose and pleasure in your life. Hope in the Lord who will give you a New Beginning, a New Joy and a New Song for your new life ahead. He promises to do you good and restore you for His own glory. (Psalm 40: 1-5)

While you may feel diminished by the death of the one you love, remember that out of that pain, God is birthing an experience of immeasurable value. (Psalm 118: 16-17). You now have the powerful truth of what it is to feel the pain of loosing a loved one.

Like Paul said in 2 Corinthians 1:3-5, as the Lord comforts you through your own sorrow, you will be better equipped to comfort and minister to those who go through this painful passage of devastating loss and grief after you. You also hold the precious knowledge of how important love can be and how vital it is as a source of joy in life – yet how easy it is to take love for granted and overlook the abundance of the love that surrounds you. Sharing that truth can greatly enlarge the lives of everyone around you.

How you actively fill your time through grief will determine whether and how your healing will occur. You will need active attention and mending. Some of the threads that will heal and mend the wound of sorrow will include forgiveness, love, creativity, sharing, relationships with others around you, etc. A healthy and positive attitude will go along way in grief recovery.

Acknowledge your feelings and grief whenever they catch up with you. Spend time with those who allow you to do so without question or judgment. Thoughtfully choose who to spend time with. Give yourself space to weep as necessary, even in private. Jesus wept when Lazarus died. (John 11:35) Your tears are a valuable reflection of the importance of the relationship that is now for ever changed.

While there is need to postpone major decisions, some things must be acted upon regularly. Enlist the help of a family member or a close trusted friend to assist you. Get clear information on insurance, paying bills, savings, debts, inheritance etc.

As time passes, take one step at a time, one day at a time prayerfully. Depending on every individual, things will become better as you learn to accept, receive support from those around you as you process your grief and start New Beginnings. Be grateful for everything you have received and experienced in your life. Be grateful for all the possibilities the future holds for you with God's grace and guidance. Begin to thank God too, for the wonderful memories you will always have of your beloved. Gratitude is an important feeling to weave into your daily life.

As you journey on, pray that every day will become an opportunity for a New Beginning to all that you will now become. Do not allow yourself to be consumed with the guilt of surviving while your loved one died. This is out of your control because God is the giver of life and has everyone's destiny and length of life.

Let the power of prayer become your best and closest companion. No matter how abandoned you will feel at times, God is present with you to the end of your life and compassionately sharing your agony.

As we learn from the words of the poem "FOOTPRINTS", when the pain and sorrow is so deep you can barely take a step, remember He promises to carry you through the deep waters or the hot fires of your sorrow and grief to a safe harbor of healing. He wants to share your burden of sorrow, walk and talk with you along the pathway of healing just like He did with His disciples on the Road to Emmaus. Just as it happened with the disciples, you may be too heart broken to notice or experience His comforting and encouraging presence at that time, but as your sorrow gradually lightens, you will realize He has truly been there for you in many places and forms.

Anchor your spirit to a solid foundation that is one with the force flowing all over the universe to touch hurting souls like yours, rest in the grace of the eternal God. Realize that your grieving is in fact, an encounter with the Eternal, that your broken heart is now an entranceway for God to abide with you. He promises you a rebirth. As your identity changes among your family and friends, your life, with God's help, can take on a new dimension, depth and texture. You can be for ever changed.

I close with the words of Paul in 2 Corinthians 4 verses 7-12.

But this precious treasure – this light and power that now shine within us – is held in perishable containers, that is, in our weak bodies. So everyone can see that our glorious power is from God and is not our own. We are pressed on every side by troubles, but we are not crushed and broken. We are perplexed, but God never abandons us. We are hunted down, but God never abandons us. We get knocked down, but we get up again and keep going.

> *Through suffering, these bodies of ours constantly share in the death of Jesus so that the life of Jesus may also be seen in our bodies.*

Psalm 118:16-17:
> *The strong right arm of the Lord is raised in triumph. The strong right arm of the Lord has done glorious things. I will not die, but I will live to tell what the Lord has done.*

This slight momentary affliction is preparing us for an eternal weight of glory beyond our imagination. As believers, we can live and lean on the hope of spending eternity with God and our dearly departed in a heaven where there will be no more ***death or sorrow or crying or pain.*** (Revelations 21:4) We will never worry about losing them to death again. The challenge now is for us to keep looking up to Jesus and to that heavenly city of God as we too continue our journey. The reality is that we too have a date with death and it matters greatly how we are living every day. The best gift we can give to those surviving us is the sure knowledge of where we are headed after we go beyond the grave. It creates hope after death and something to hang on to.

The sudden or even expected death (from prolonged terminal illness) and the absence of a spouse of many years might leave one feeling as if they are in a non-ending whirlpool of life. No matter how large or small our outside is, we often come to see our partner as the primary source and resource – the one we turn to for acknowledgement, affirmation and comfort, etc. Death in these relationships overturns one's life. Dinnertime or evening

times might have become the sundowner that is suddenly discontinued without any prior notice. Career and social ups and downs was a staple of nightly briefing moments or during the pillow-talk. All manner of loss or gain were generally shared. The person you turned to every time your heart hurt is no longer there for you. Your spouse's death is now the source of the deepest pain you have ever experienced. You are now wondering and fearful of who and where to turn to. Who can even understand what you are really going through?

The death of one's long-term spouse leaves one feeling as if they have literary lost a piece of their own body. Similar heartache and pain might also be provoked by divorce or separation after many years of marriage. The emotions attached to a death or divorce is not defined by time but by the feelings they produced within time. The grieving spouse is suddenly wrapped up in grief and the frightening thought of raising children alone or growing old alone.

It is a common observation that women handle their grief better and remain unmarried for longer or for the rest of their lives. Men often bottle up their grief and behave heroic. On the other hand, older widowers and widows might be ridiculed for dating or remarrying. People tend to forget that even in their senior years, they too need intimacy. Their children also at times go into shock and disbelief forgetting that their widowed parent has needs (emotional, spiritual, sexual etc). However, it is important for the surviving parent to be considerate of the children bearing in mind that they too have lost their father.

Find an appropriate way of sharing your intentions and give them a chance to meet this person you intend to make part of their lives. Allow them some time alone to experience each other. Whether young or old, help your children and family understand that your remarrying does not imply that you did not love their father or mother. On the other hand, if this new person cannot cope with your children, it would be advisable to reevaluate the situation. It is worth remembering that your children will be a part of your life for as long as you live.

At the same time, society is more permissive and understanding towards men than women and will be less criticized if they remarry. Befriending a common friend between the deceased spouse and the grieving spouse will often result in scandals, with suspicion that this relationship might have existed even before the death. In all fairness, no widow or widower should be punished for remarrying and moving on with their lives. It is their life. No one should have the right to make them feel guilty for new found love. There is no "proper" length of grieving time before remarrying either after the death of a spouse or a divorce. The priority and the determining factor should be one's own happiness, not necessarily pleasing others. If there are children, it is wise to reason with them as best as humanly possible, but you have the final word.

Nobody should be compelled to mourn or pay a tribute to a lost life for ever. Some people may enter into a new relationship immediately to help cope with their grief and avoid loneliness and isolation. Too soon may cause its own complications as the mind of the grieving person may still be intensely wrapped around their grief, hampering their capacity to make good decisions or relate comfortably with others. At such times when the grieving person is still very vulnerable, they might easily expose themselves to ill intentioned predators who might take advantage of them.

Build a new "normal" life for yourself.

You know yourself and your coping strengths better than anyone else. As hard as this may be, remember that even though your life companion has passed away, your future was not wiped away. You still have a future, just that it has been somewhat altered from your original path and hopes laid down by you and your late spouse.

Face your emotions.

Grief brings real and not imaginary fears that you cannot simply ignore or wish away. Cry whenever you need to. This is your personal journey of tears and nobody can or should dictate to you on how to process your stress.

Find new friends

As a widow or widower, you might feel uncomfortable and unable to fit into the social circles you enjoyed when your spouse lived. This may be true in some cases, but some of your former comrades might still want to keep up with you and to be in your support system. However, look for widowed people's support group who will understand you and your emotions better. Such support groups may be found in churches, hospitals, hospices and counseling organizations.

Be Safe

As you interact with other people, you will be reassured, encouraged and strengthened. As you depend on God and faith, you will feel stronger and gradually in control of your life again which also helps. Rely on your spirituality as much as possible and let God's love and grace heal, nurture and restore you.

Discover yourself:

However long or short you have lived with your spouse, his absence from your life may leave you feeling very vulnerable in many ways. Insecurity and fear creep in. Allow yourself to take up new responsibilities previously handled by your late spouse gradually. This may include lawn care, plumbing, simple repairs, planning your finances or family holidays. If you feel overwhelmed, feel free to ask for help when necessary instead of suddenly overloading your grieving mind. You will be surprised at how many people are eager to help you but are afraid to offer lest they appear as if they are imposing themselves on you. With time, you will feel better, more confident and happier. Do not allow yourself to feel guilty of all the improvements you are making, but keep the good memories of your spouse and imagine how proud he/she would be to see you doing better.

Imagine the worst

Instead of fretting and panicking about what *may* happen, think what worse could be. You would still survive. It may take changing your lifestyle to cut down on expenses. It may even necessitate selling some things you no longer need in order to keep up with your bills and other financial responsibilities. That may be okay too. Remember the Serenity Prayer. Ask God to help you change what you can and to accept what you cannot change. Do what you have to do and constantly seek God's help and guidance in every step and need.

Encourage yourself in God:

He promises never to leave or forsake you. He also promises in Isaiah 43:19 that he will make a way in the sea. He will also do a new thing in your life.

You never forget. You will carry your beloved with you for ever as a cherished part of who you are, and grow to be more compassionate, appreciative and more tolerant with other people. As you keep facing your fears, you will learn to embrace life again, connecting, laughing and loving again with a full heart.

Grieving the Loss of a Parent:

When you lose a parent, you lose your past.

The loss of a parent, regardless of how old or young one is, must be one of the most disorienting losses. Whether one has been brought up by both parent or by a single parent, the intensity of losing a parent can be devastating. This is the first person(s) that a baby ever gets into contact with before and after birth. These are the first voices, faces and touch that the baby experiences and bonds with that represent security, safety, unconditional love and protection. And even as we mature and grow older, our parents remain a pillar of strength and support in the midst of the storms of life. These are the first people we turn to for affirmation and appreciation. One's parent(s) tend to become a constant point of contact even for those who travel around the world, even into the battlefields all over the world. It is one's parent who will be there to celebrate us when we succeed and support us when we are in trouble. It is not unusual to find that the only people, who are present in a murder or other serious criminal trials, when everyone else has given up, are one's parents. The parent will continue standing by their child even after they are judged and committed to life imprisonment or even to a death-row for their crimes. It is our parents who love us when everyone else give up and want nothing to do with us.

The reality therefore is that when a parent dies, one feels lost and wondering what next, especially for young children still dependent on their parents. Even for adults, it is still hard because we still seek advice and approval from them. There is a deep sense of loss and emptiness knowing that while one can remarry after the loss of a spouse, or have other children after the loss of a child, we have only one biological father and mother in a lifetime. This is not in any way to suggest that you can easily replace either a spouse or a child, but that one can have more than one.

I thought it was tragic enough to lose my two younger brothers, especially as I agonized on what it did to my parents who were still alive. But the death of both parents within 4 months is still the worst grief that I have ever experienced. Odd as it sounds coming from a mature grandmother, I suddenly realized what it feels to be an orphan. I had already gone through a divorce and my parents stood for and with me through the worst situations of my life. They were my heroes in many ways. As I struggled with many life issues, it was the assurance from my father and my mother that they believed in me and were praying for me, that propelled me forward to surviving different crises. I was able to bounce back into life after crashing blows of life as long as my mother was around. I had learnt to trust her with every bit of my life and could confidently bear my struggles and failures without fearing rejection. But for now, I am continuously leaning on the sweet comforting memories of my mother and the nurturing empowering words she told me over the years. As I reminisce on her memories, her strength, values, principles and most of all her faith, telling her stories, I feel comforted as if she is close-by.

As we grieve and miss our parents, it will help to remember some funny moments shared as we were growing up, some heroic deeds in a challenging situation and thank God for them. Perhaps you remember a father sharing something that influenced you and changed your general outlook to life in a moment of great challenge like the loss of a job, a broken relationship or even starting your own family. If he motivated you to move on, thank God for that and use that memory and draw strength from that to move on. It may even be a challenge he gave you to do something you never imagined you could ever do. Your parents might have been the recharging elements whenever you felt like your energies were fading off and you wanted to quit. Let such memories propel you upwards, however slowly it feels. Try to imagine them still cheering you as they did during whatever games you enjoyed with them. Imagine them standing by your bedside praying as you awaited some surgical procedures. I felt some deep sense of peace a little while after my mother died and I had to undergo a major back surgery. At one point I wished she was there like she always did at such moments in her lifetime, praying for me before surgery. I found comfort in remembering and believing that she would always be with me in the spirit ***wherever and whenever*** I yearned for her.

In a case where a parent(s) were either sick or well advanced in age, we may be called to love them deeply enough to want what is good for them even though it may not be good for us. I am thinking of the many times I have been called to support families whose parent is fast declining and every indication shows they will not recover. Sometimes dealing with that reality and with doctors suggesting they need to let the doctors stop the life support so that the parent can rest in peace from what is ailing them. I have found this to be the hardest decision anyone is ever asked to make for a loved one, not just a parent but everyone. This is worse still if the dying person has no living will stating clearly what they would want done for them in such a moment. This is a moment when one is called to overlook your interest of having your parent with you for as long as possible and let them rest out of their sick body and go back to their heavenly home

Unfortunately, their being very old does not exempt us from the pain of losing them to death. There will never be a time when we are completely ready for their absence from our lives. But it calls on those surviving them to be considering what is good for the dying parent and allow God to do His will and take them to their final resting place if the time comes. Life then challenges you, as with all other deaths and loses to adapt to a new life and journey without your parents. The Lord who knows our end from the very beginning will continue to guide and direct our lives long after our parents have gone out of our lives. This may sound impossible when a baby or a young child is left without one or both parents at a very tender age, but one way or the other, God will in His own way ensure that their destiny will be lived as He originally planned for them. Our lives will have to move on, even though drastically altered by the absence of our parents.

When we know and fully understand our own emotional journey, its challenges and the recovering process we will handle our transition in a better and more confident manner. However, when we lose our parents under some tragic unexpected circumstances, accidents, our healing process is definitely altered, complicated and harder to bear. The death of any parent with whom we had good relationships, crashes and breaks our hearts in a way we cannot imagine surviving. It removes all the safety and security we have ever known. To a certain extent, especially in young children, death steals trust, confidence and freedom. This brings back to memory sadness and sorrow for things and people who had died long ago, like grandparents and other close relatives.

As you watch you parents mourn their own parents, you realize that their sorrow was separated only by the tissue of time from what would some day be your sorrow for the loss of your own parents. Part of the grief you feel for your grandparents will be your own anticipatory grief as you wonder how you would survive the death of your own parents whenever it happens. Sometimes it sensitizes people to be careful how they treat their own parents. Suddenly people realize that their parents are also advanced in age and could be gone sooner than later. This is more evident when you lose a grownup sibling and observe the way it completely crashes your parents as they mourn their child who should have survived them. Like in the case of my parents, the death of my second younger brother seemed to be the last straw as we heard our parents say they would not want to live through such an experience again. It seemed to take their motivation to live and they slowly declined in health and both died two years after that.

It may be that you also hear of the death of their age-mates or attend funerals. This puts you through a mental prelude of imagining your parents in similar coffins, images of them dead and even the awful big grave. You begin to have some very vivid imaginations of what might happen to them and what that would mean for you. But when death finally strikes home, all these imaginations are poor and insignificant in the face of the final sufferings and agony of your deep grief and loss.

As your parent(s) takes their last breath, the final layer of your childhood is discontinued for ever. As hard as it is to see them go and perhaps you being called to speak at their funeral, certain thoughts and memories will challenge your silent grief. There will be some things known only to you about them that need to be said in their honor which will land squarely on you to honor them as they are laid to their final resting place. This may be the hardest thing you will ever have to do, but many have said finally they were glad they did that and it gave them an inner peace that also helped come to terms with their parent's death. I can attest to that feeling, having preached at my own mother's memorial service. It was a very emotional thing but I had to honor her request. It is a rare and last chance to stand and redeem your parent's heroic ordinary life. Some feel it is a one last chance to show our parents, family and friends that we can be counted on to stand up for them and carry on their legacy.

Despite of all that is going on, suddenly we discover and realize that we have actually grown up and endured one of the worst heartaches – the death of a parent like many others before you. Other people experience the transformation of life that comes with the grief and loss of a parent. Prayerfully, you must take over the baton from them and continue the race of life from generation to generation. This reminds us of our mortality and the fact that we are now the link between the receding generations to newly developing generations after us.

Apparently, looking at what has happened around our parent's death, one feels the urge to put your own life/house in order. This is especially important if you have a spouse and children. You analyze any and all decisions that might have been left hanging like the Living Will, you main will, etc. If you were personally challenged by these upon your parent's death on top of your deep grief, you will want to ensure that your own family would not have to deal with that upon your own death. This is often referred to as ensuring that you lay clear stepping stones for those who come after you. Do things that would make it easier for your own family and friends in their grieving process. As much as we desire to do a celebration of the life of those that have gone before us, complications from unfinished businesses might make this very hard.

As in any other loses, find ways of remembering your parents and keeping their memories alive for future generations. Depending on the ability of the surviving families, there are many ways of honoring the departed. You can donate to charity in their honor, establishing a foundation or project in memory of them, etc. Find a way of sharing their stories and their achievements. Continue to sustain any projects they started in their lifetime and strive to complete any that they were still working on. Acknowledge the sadness, the fear, the uncertainty you might be experiencing because of this grief and loss. If it is prolonged, seek professional counseling to help you through this phase. Find a grief support group and if necessary one that specifically deals with the loss of a parent. You will find people who can identify with you, empathize with you and walk through the path of grief with you. Gradually, however long or short, the grief may become bearable and you will start reliving the good memories of things you enjoyed doing together with your parent.

While I still miss my father, I am at a point where I thank God for him and remember the many times as I went through my own struggles, and my father's constant affirmation reminding me that he had great confidence in my surviving whatever I was undergoing and coming out victorious because he and my mother were praying for me. I can almost hear his firm voice reminding me that "Penny, you know quitting is not an option for you". Because of his faith in me and wanting so much to honor that, I found myself overcoming challenges I had thought would finish me.

I remember my mother forcing me to sing the "Amazing Grace" with her in the midst of major storms in our lives, and reminding me that God's grace was as fresh and real for me as it was for Paul. One way of experiencing my mother's efforts and God's control. He wants us to use our minds, to seek the advice of others, and to plan. Nevertheless, the results are up to Him. Planning then, helps us act God's way. As the Christian Entrepreneur lives for Him, ask for guidance as you plan, and then act on your plan as you trust in Him.

<u>Things To Remember</u>

1. Write a goals statement.

2. Does the goal sufficiently meet the Christian Entrepreneur's needs?

3. Is the goal positively stated? If not, rewrite it.

4. Is the goal under the Christian Entrepreneur's control?

5. Does the goal focus on the Christian Entrepreneur's actions and no one else's?

6. Is the goal an actual goal, and not a result?

7. Is the goal important enough to the Christian Entrepreneur that he/she will want to work toward achieving it? Does he/she have the time and energy to do it?

8. How will this goal make the Christian Entrepreneur's life different?

9. What barriers might the Christian Entrepreneur encounter in working toward this goal?

10. Is the goal skill based?

Chapter 6

THE CHRISTIAN ENTREPRENEUR & AMBITION

Ambition means having a strong desire for success or achievement, it's something that requires the full use of your abilities or resources; it's performing the most challenging task without a mistake. It's possessing, or controlled by, greatly or inordinately desirous of power, honor, office, superiority, or distinction; strongly desirous.

The best type of ambition is when the ambition source becomes the desire to reach a big goal or to fulfill your life purpose. Aiming for something big for the sake of making a big change is the best type of ambition that you can have because it's not rooted to self doubts nor is it rooted to concerns about your image in front of others.

God You Said....
- He who has a slack hand becomes poor, but the hand of the diligent makes rich, he who gathers in summer is a wise son; he who sleeps in harvest is a son who causes shame. *(Proverbs 10:4-5)*

The Christian Entrepreneur should not think that God's promised provision is meant to encourage sloth and idleness, for diligence in our labor is God's means of giving us our needs. Someone has wisely observed that God generally gives most to the most diligent and most faithful workers. Parallel teaching is found in Proverbs 13:4 and 19:15. Hard labor has been man's decreed lot since he sinned in Eden, (Gen. 3:17-19), but it can be blessed to the enrichment of man by the Lord, where a man's ways please the Lord. All attempts to get rich without honest labor are simply man's denial of his sinfulness, and his attempt to bypass the curse. Labor is meant to remind man of his sinfulness.

No one lives unto himself, and the child that causes shame, not only is dishonored himself, but he also dishonors his parents who have taught him. In this proverb, wisdom is shown to include planning ahead.

God You Said....
- The soul of a lazy man desires, and has nothing; but the soul of the diligent shall be made rich. *(Proverbs 13:4)*

Hard work and diligence produce both material gain and moral character.

God You Said....
- The plans of the diligent lead surely to plenty, but those of everyone who is hasty, surely to poverty. *(Proverbs 21:5)*

Faithful completion of mundane tasks is a great accomplishment. Such work is patiently carried out according to a plan. Diligence does not come naturally to most people; it is a result of strong character. Don't look for quick and easy answers. Be a diligent servant to God in your business.

God You Said....
- Do you see a man who excels in his work? He will stand before kings, he will not stand before unknown men. *(Proverbs 22:29)*

The destiny of the diligent is not the company of the obscure and insignificant.

God You Said....
- Be diligent to know the state of your flocks, and attend to your herds. *(Proverbs 27:23)*

Know the state of your flocks refers to diligence in record keeping. In modern times, this means keeping track of what we own, owe, earn, and spend.

God You Said....

- Whatever your hands find to do, do it with your might; for there is no work or device or knowledge or wisdom in the grave where you are going. *(Ecclesiastes 9:10)*

The Christian Entrepreneur should do everything they undertake with all of their strength.

God You Said....

- Let your light so shine before men, that they may see your good works and glorify your Father in heaven. *(Matthew 5:16)*

The Christian Entrepreneurs are to let their lights shine by letting the marketplace see the good works that God's grace has produced in their businesses, thus directing attention to God's saving power.

God You Said....

- Command those who are rich in this present age not to be haughty, nor to trust in uncertain riches, but in the living God, who gives us richly all things to enjoy. *(1 Timothy 6:17)*

Paul advises Timothy to deal with any potential problems by teaching that having riches carries great responsibility. Those who have money must be generous, but they may not be arrogant just because they have a lot to give. They must be careful not to put their hope in money instead of in the living God for their security. Even if we don't have material wealth, we can be rich in good works. No matter how poor we are, we have something to share with someone.

God You Said....

- A man's gift makes room for him, and brings him before great men. *(Proverbs 18:16)*

This gift is not a bribe, but an asset or talent which opens the way.

Seven Habits of Ambitious Christian Entrepreneurs

1. **Ambitious Christian Entrepreneurs - Have big ideas**

   They have a clear, plausible, optimistic vision of the future. Employees and customers can describe what the company is *for* in simple terms. They set big, ambitious goals. They thrive on change but stay true to their purpose. They use their big idea to define their strategy.

2. **Ambitious Christian Entrepreneurs - Stay focused**

   They are flexible about means but constant about objectives. They have a bias for action, for analysis without paralysis, for delegation. Whether they diversify or specialize, they make smart business decisions and back winners.

3. **Ambitious Christian Entrepreneurs - Build momentum**

   They make smart, timely decisions. They remove obstacles to productivity and have fewer, shorter meetings. They don't let the impossible interfere with the possible.

4. **Ambitious Christian Entrepreneurs - Put people first**

   Ambitious companies hire ambitious people. They maximize their return on people with training, meritocracy, flexible working, and respect. The interests of shareholders, management and employees aligned. They give people the tools and information they need to do the job. They are unapologetic about going after the best talent available.

5. **Ambitious Christian Entrepreneurs - Encourage communication**

   They start by listening: to customers, employees and critics alike. They encourage blogging. They speak clearly with a distinctive voice. They sound like people, not like lawyers.

6. **Ambitious Christian Entrepreneurs - Manage innovation**

They run a portfolio of R&D investments, mixing the safe with the revolutionary. They don't punish failure to succeed, only failure to try.

7. **Ambitious Christian Entrepreneurs - Listen to their conscience**

They have an environmental and social conscience and listen to it. Not because they have to, but because it makes good business sense.

Chapter 7

THE CHRISTIAN ENTREPRENEUR & STRENGTH

Strength is defined as the quality or state of being strong; it's the ability to do or to bear; it's the power of resisting attack, capacity for exertion or endurance, solidity, one regarded as embodying or affording force or firmness, toughness, whether physical, intellectual, or moral; force; vigor; power; as, body or of the arm; strength of mind, of memory, or of judgment.

Strength requires motivation, determination, confidence and will power. As Christian Entrepreneurs we are tested to the limits every day in terms of our belief and courage. But where do we get the strength from? Was it something our mother's or father's said to us that makes us fight to the death or do we just have something to prove to ourselves? No, the answer is very simple, the Christian Entrepreneurs strength comes from the Lord.

God You Said.....
*   Do not sorrow, for the joy of the Lord is your strength. *(Nehemiah 8:10B)*

The Christian Entrepreneur who is joyful will acquire *strength* and their minds power and fervour, so that they will be able to do God's will in their business, and to do it *cheerfully. Religious joy,* that is properly tempered with continual dependence on the help of God, meekness of mind, and self-diffidence, is a powerful means of strengthening the Christian Entrepreneur. In such a state, every duty is practicable, and every duty delightful. In such a frame of mind no Christian Entrepreneur can ever fell, and in such a state of mind the general health of the **Body of Christ** is much improved; a cheerful heart is not only a continual feast, but also a continual medicine. The Christian Entrepreneur must cultivate and promote the joy of the Lord among God's people, which is a powerful source of spiritual strength.

God You Said.....
- Be of good courage, and He shall strengthen your heart, all you who hope in the Lord. (*Psalm 31:24*)

The Christian Entrepreneur that has hope in God, and is endeavoring to walk carefully before him, may take courage at all times, and expect the fullness of the blessing of the Gospel of peace.

God You Said.....
- A wise man is strong, yes, a man of knowledge increases strength. (*Proverbs 24:5*)

The Christian Entrepreneur who thinks-who assesses the situation and plans strategies-has an advantage over a physically stronger, but unthinking opponent. And wisdom, not muscle, is certainly why God has put His people in charge of the marketplace. We exercise regularly and eat well to build our strength, but do we take equal pains to develop wisdom? Since wisdom is a vital part of strength, it pays to attain it.

God You Said.....
- I can do all things through Christ who strengthens me. (*Philippians 4:13*)

For the Christian Entrepreneur, it is important to note that the emphasis is not so much on achievement as it is on the willingness to allow Christ's power to sustain in difficulty and scarcity, and to enhance the enjoyment of abundance and prosperity. Such faith is a stimulant for the Christian Entrepreneur to believe for all Christ's sufficiency in facing all life's circumstances.

God You Said....

- The name of the Lord is a strong tower; the righteous run to it and are safe. *(Proverbs 18:10)*

Through all the adversity that takes place in the Christian Entrepreneur's business, he or she must know that the name of the Lord is a strong tower, a refuge, and place of complete safety, to all that trust in Him. The Christian Entrepreneur has to know and believe that Lord will always take care of His followers.

God You Said....

- My help comes from the Lord, who made heaven and earth. *(Psalm 121:2)*

There is no help for the Christian Entrepreneur but in God; and they should expect it from no other source.

God You Said....

- He gives power to the weak, And to those who have no might He increases strength. (*Isaiah 40:29*)

For the Christian Entrepreneur who is ready to faint under afflictions, because they do not have immediate results, or their prayers are not answered at once, or promises not fulfilled as they expected; to such He gives fresh supplies of spiritual strength; He strengthens their faith, and enlarges their views. Not that the Christian Entrepreneur does not have no might at all, strictly speaking; for then it could not be properly said their strength was increased by Him; but that their might and power were very small, and that in their own apprehensions they had none, and then it is that fresh strength that is given to them; as the apostle says, "when I am weak, then am I strong"; 2 Corinthians 12:10. May the Lord increase your spiritual strength.

God You Said....

- Don't be afraid, the prophet answered, "Those who are with us are more than those who are with them." *(2 Kings 6:16)*

The Christian Entrepreneur who has a strong relationship with heaven, will have the whole heavenly host there commissioned to help him on his entrepreneurial journey.

God You Said....

- For God has not given us a spirit of fear, but of power and of love and of a sound mind. (*2 Timothy 1:7*)

God has not given the Christian Entrepreneur a spirit of fear; but of power, to work miracles, to confound enemies, to support us in trials, and enable us to do that which is lawful and right in His sight. And of love, which enables us the Christian Entrepreneur to hear, believe, hope, and endure all things; and is the incentive to all obedience. Of a sound mind, which means a clear understanding, a sound judgment, and a rectified will. The apostle says, God has given the spirit of these things; they are not factitious; they are not assumed for times and circumstances; they are radical powers and tempers; each produced by its proper principle.

God You Said....

- My soul melts from heaviness; strengthen me according to Your word. *(Psalm 119:28)*

The word of God strengthens our faith, and builds us up. The Word of God can be relied upon, with confidence. Meditate on, and rely upon, the Word of God. Saturate your mind and your spirit with the Word, and the promises of the Word, for your strengthening. As we do these things, God will impart His strength to us. The Christian Entrepreneur will be strengthened to walk in victory, and walk in faith. God will show Himself strong on our behalf. At times God's people can begin to drift, and begin to coast along on their own strength. We can gradually begin to do things in our own strength, and not even realize that we are no longer walking in the strength of the Lord. That is why we must seek fresh strength from the Lord day by day and week by week. We must seek fresh strength in prayer, the Word, and waiting upon the Lord. The Israelites in the wilderness so often missed God's purposes. God wanted to make them strong - strong in faith, strong in trust, strong in the Lord. But when food and water began to run low, they didn't feel strong; they felt weaker. They missed God's purpose - He wanted to strengthen them, and provide for all of their needs. But they often doubted, or grumbled and complained. God's ways were higher than their ways. The Christian Entrepreneur must always press forward.

God You Said....

- In quietness and in confidence shall be your strength. *(Isaiah 30:15)*

For the Christian Entrepreneur to be strengthened, it must be in quietness and in confidence, keeping peace in their own minds, and relying upon God. Those who make God alone their confidence, will have comfort. Our strength comes from God as we trust in Him. And as we trust in Him, we learn to wait for Him. And when we wait for Him, He blesses us. Finding rest in our Savior is the only way the Christian Entrepreneur will be saved from the hectic in their business. God ever waits to be gracious to all that come to Him by faith in Christ, and happy are those who wait (trust) for Him.

God You Said....

- But they that wait upon the Lord shall renew their strength; they shall mount up with wings as eagles; they shall run, and not be weary; and they shall walk, and not faint. *(Isaiah 40:31)*

Acknowledged weakness is the first step in receiving God's enabling power. One of the most magnificent sights of the wild is an eagle soaring in the sky, higher and higher, with seemingly little effort. Similarly, the Christian Entrepreneur who draws his strength from above is not only enabled to go ever onward and upward, but higher and still higher to achieve the goals which come into view. When Christian Entrepreneurs run like champions on God's mission, they then should give God the glory for all He accomplishes through them.

God You Said....

- Finally, my brethren, be strong in the Lord, and in the power of His might. *(Ephesians 6:10)*

The Almighty God has laid before the Christian Entrepreneur their great and high calling, from there God will show the Christian Entrepreneur the enemies that will oppose them, and the strength which is requisite to enable the Christian Entrepreneur to repel them. For the Christian Entrepreneur to be strong in the Lord, they must have strength, and strength of a spiritual kind, and such spiritual strength only can come from the Lord Himself. The Christian Entrepreneur must have this strength through an indwelling God, which is the power of His might working in you.

God You Said....

- If you faint in the day of adversity, your strength is small. *(Proverbs 24:10)*

If the Christian Entrepreneur give way to discouragement and despair in the day of adversity, time of trial or temptation. Their strength is small. In times of trials the Christian Entrepreneur should endeavor to be doubly courageous; when a Christian Entrepreneur loses his or her courage, their strength avails them nothing.

God You Said....

- Wait on the Lord; be of good courage; and He shall strengthen your heart; wait, I say, on the Lord! *(Psalm 27:14)*

Wait On Lord:

The Christian Entrepreneur is told to wait on the Lord, spend time with Him, wait on the Lord for the common blessings for your business, for even the eyes of all wait upon Him, but He will return at the set time; and provide answers for your prayers, which will be given sooner or later. His promises will be performed, which are yes and amen in Christ.

Be of good courage:

The Christian Entrepreneur has need of courage, considering the enemies they have to grapple with in the marketplace along with Satan, and his principalities and powers; and men of the world, and they have great reason, notwithstanding, to be of good courage, since God is for them; Christ is the Captain of their salvation; the Holy Spirit, that is in them, is greater than he that is in the world; they have angels encamp around them and they are engaged in a good cause and are sure of victory.

God You Said....

• Put on the whole armor of God, that you may be able to stand against the wiles of the devil. (*Ephesians 6:11*)

The Christian Entrepreneur does not oppose evil in his own strength, but in the strength of the Lord. Only the armor of God is sufficient to the warfare involved. This refers to the stratagems employed by the evil one with the design of destroying the faith of the Christian Entrepreneur. The battle is the Lord's.

Things To Remember

1. Strength is what you need to become a successful entrepreneur.

2. Strength is what you call upon when the going gets tough.

3. Strength is all you have when you are filled with doubt.

4. Strength is what it takes to overcome adversity.

5. Strength requires motivation - and will power.

Chapter 8

THE CHRISTIAN ENTREPRENEUR
& THE ABUNDANT LIFE

The abundant life means being fully alive; not dying but living & living eternally with fullness, completeness, with great quantity, richly supplied, plentiful, extensive, bountiful, and rich. For the Christian Entrepreneur, it means serving Jesus Christ first, then serving your family and then working unto the Lord.

Are you living in God's abundance? The abundant life is Christ living His life out in you and you surrendering your life to Christ to allow spiritual growth. God's grace and power is sufficient for every need that the Christian Entrepreneur might encounter.

The abundant life assures the Christian Entrepreneur that he or she can experience God's blessings in this life and heaven, too. They can enter into the abundant life today and experience the joy of the Lord. God created the Christian Entrepreneur to be happy, healthy, and whole.

God's Word is forever established in heaven (Psalm 119:89) and is living, powerful, and sharper than any two-edged sword, piercing even to the dividing of soul and spirit, and of both joints and marrow, and is able to discern the thoughts and intentions of the heart (Hebrews 4:12).

His Word contains the power you need to bring outrageous blessings into your life! But, before His Word can bring outrageous blessings into your life, you must first believe that it can. You must also believe that He is a God of abundance, and that it is His will that you live an abundant and prosperous life.

God You Said....

- The thief does not come except to steal, and to kill and to destroy, I have come that they may have life, and that they may have it more abundantly. *(John 10:10)*

The word abundantly, in the Greek is perissos (per-is-soss); Strong's #4053: means superabundance, excessive, overflowing, surplus, over and above, more than enough, profuse, extraordinary, above the ordinary, more than sufficient.

God's covenant to us is a covenant for abundant life. From the very beginning of time, Scripture shows us that God wanted us to be happy and prosperous. In the Book of Genesis, we are told that God made everything and declared it to be good. Then He gave this beautiful, plentiful Earth to Adam; Adam was given dominion over all of it (Genesis 1:28). God's plan from the beginning was for man to be enriched and to have a prosperous, abundant life. Here Jesus declares His intention to recover and restore to man what was the Father's intent and to break and block the Devil's intent to hinder our receiving it.

God You Said....

- I know how to be abased, and I know how to abound. Everywhere and in all things I have learned both to be full and to be hungry, both abound and to suffer need. I can do all things through Christ who strengthens me. *(Philippians 4:12-13)*

The Christian Entrepreneur should note that the emphasis is not so much on achievement as it is on willingness to allow Christ's power to sustain in difficulty and scarcity, and to enhance the enjoyment of abundance and prosperity. Such faith is a stimulant to believe for all Christ's sufficiency in facing all life's circumstances. The Christian Entrepreneur needs to learn to be content in all circumstances. Contentment will bring great freedom to your life and to your business.

God You Said....

- Now the Lord has said to Abram: "Get out of your country, from your family and from your father's house; to a land that I will show you. I will make you a great nation; I will bless you and make your name great; and you shall be a blessing. I will bless those who bless you, and I will curse him who curses you; and in you all the families of the earth shall be blessed." *(Genesis 12:1-3)*

In this passage, God promises to make Abraham great; and God did bless Abraham in many ways, including material blessings. Genesis 13:1-2 is where we see how Abraham was made very wealthy. Also see Genesis 24:35, where Abraham's servant reports that "the Lord has blessed my master greatly," this enumerates the material blessings that God had given to Abraham. The dynamic of this historic fact becomes pertinent to every Christian Entrepreneur today. We are Abraham's seed, and God promised Abraham that all his seeds would be blessed. This allows the Christian Entrepreneur to move in the marketplace with great confidence.

In Galatians 3:13-14, God promises to give all believers the blessing of Abraham, telling us that Jesus became a curse for us so that we might receive "the blessing of Abraham." This begins, of course, with our being born again, or becoming new creatures in Christ Jesus. But "the blessing of Abraham" involves other areas as well. The Lord wants us to prosper spiritually, emotionally and physically, and materially. Abraham's blessing is ours by His promise, and we need to make no apology for the fact that prosperity is included.

God You Said....

- Will a man rob God? Yet you have robbed Me! But you say, in what way have we robbed You? In tithes and offerings. You are cursed with a curse, for you have robbed Me, even this whole nation. Bring all the tithes into the storehouse, That there may be food in My house, and try Me now in this, says the Lord of hosts, if I will not open for you the windows of heaven and pour out for you such blessing that there will not be room enough to receive it. And I will rebuke the devourer for your sakes, So that he will not destroy the fruit of your ground, nor shall the vine fail to bear fruit for you in the field, says the Lord of hosts. *(Malachi 3:8-11)*

God actually invites people to try (prove) Him-to verify His trustworthiness with their giving. He says that by withheld giving we rob Him of the privilege of pouring out great and overflowing blessings. He calls for renewed giving with this promise. First, there will be "food" or resources for God's work ("in My house"). Second, He says those who give will be placed in position to receive great, overflowing blessings. Third, God says that He will "rebuke the devourer" for your sakes. Satan himself cannot stop it. Nothing will keep a wise Christian Entrepreneur from tithing and giving, but he or she will never be found to tithe or give offerings just to get something in return. Rather, the act arises from obedience, and God always rewards obedience. Do not be afraid to prove God with your giving; He is God, and He will stand the test every time.

God You Said....

* Give and it will be given to you: good measure, pressed down, shaken together, and running over will be put into your bosom. For with the same measure that you use, it will be measured back to you. *(Luke 6:38)*

One key way to Christian Entrepreneurial success is Jesus' call "to give, and it will be given." Financial obstacles tempt us to give up, but instead God's Word call us to give away. True Christian Entrepreneurship always involves coming to terms with our human tendency to clutch things to ourselves, especially material belongings. Jesus exemplifies the essence of "giving by sowing your own life" – your own interests. This pathway of yielding up all to Him often calls us to give when we ourselves may be in need. It seems counterproductive, but giving out of our own need is God's way of clearing the avenues for heaven's abounding toward His purposes for ministry and service that He wants to send into the Earth realm through us, the Christian Entrepreneur.

The Law of Devine Reciprocity

There is a universal law of divine reciprocity. You give; God gives in return. When you plant a seed, the ground yields a harvest. That is a reciprocal relationship. The ground can only give to you as you give to the ground. You put money in the bank, and the bank returns interest. That is reciprocity. But many people want something for nothing when it comes to the things of God. They know that it does not work that way in the world system. Yet they always expect God to send them something when they have not invested in the Kingdom of God. If you are not investing your time, talent, commitment, and your money, why do you want something? How can you get something when you have not planted any seed? How can you expect God to honor your desire when you have not honored His command to give? Abundance begins with investment.

God Expects You to Receive a Harvest from Your Giving

Jesus opened up a whole new way of giving. We can no longer pay or sacrifice our way into God's mercy. Jesus Christ has paid our debt before God, and His Cross is a completed work in our eternal interest. Our giving, then, is no longer a debt that we owe, but a seed that we sow! The life and power source is from Him. Ours is simply to act on the power potential in that seed-life He has placed in us by His power and grace! Notice that when Jesus said, "Give," He also said, "and it will be given to you." Giving and receiving belong together. Only when we give are we in a position to expect to reach out and receive a harvest. And Jesus said the harvest will be "good measure, pressed down, shaken together, and running over."

God You Said....

• Do not be deceived, God is not mocked; for whatever a man sows, that he will also reap. For he who sows to his flesh will of the flesh reap corruption, but he who sows to the Spirit will of the Spirit reap everlasting life. And let us not grow weary while doing good, for in due season we shall reap if we do not lose heart. **(Galatians 6:7-9)**

God has a timetable for every seed we plant. His timetable is not always our timetable. Sometimes the "due season" means a quick return. Sometimes it means a slow return that may take years –

even a lifetime. But we can count on three things. First, God will cause a harvest to come from our seeds. Second, God is never early or late – He is right on time with our best interests at heart. Third, our harvest will have the same nature as our seeds sown; good seeds bring good harvest, bad seeds bring bad harvest.

What are we to do during the growing time of our seeds? 1). Refuse to become discourage. 2). Determine to keep your faith alive and active. 3). Give and keep on giving; love and keep on loving. Know this – a harvest is guaranteed. The Christian Entrepreneur must continue in an attitude of expectancy.

The Promise of Harvest
The passion for God to move among His people sometimes seems slow in being rewarded. Sincere Christian Entrepreneurs often labor, pray, and seek fruitfulness for extended seasons before the visitation of God's grace bringing the long-sought harvest. This text may apply many ways, but to the earnest Christian Entrepreneur, the call is, "Do not lose heart; harvest is certain." Spirit-directed words, actions, giving, serving, and loving are all good seeds. God has promised to multiply those good seeds back to you. There is a due season-wait for it!

God You Said….
- And God is able to make all grace abound toward you, that you, always having all sufficiency in all things, may have an abundance for every good work. As it is written: "He has dispersed abroad, He has given to the poor, His righteousness endures forever." Now may He who supplies seed to the sower, and bread for food, supply and multiply the seed you have sown and increase the fruits of your righteousness. *(2 Corinthians 9:8-10)*

Give What You Have in Your Hand to Give
The Christian Entrepreneur needs to note especially these three things as you study this passage. First, God is the One who makes all grace abound toward you and provides sufficiency in all things. All things beneficial for our lives come from God's hands. Second, we are given sufficiency – even "bounty" so that we might do good

works. We are blessed in order to be a blessing to others! The word "sufficiency" means "contentedness," or "competence" – earmarks of the Christian Entrepreneur believer whose life is truly blessed by these characteristics as God increases him. And third, the God who gave you the seed in the first place is the One who meets your basic needs, multiplies your seed sown into an abundance so that you can share with others, and increases you spiritually with love, joy, peace, and all of the other fruits Spirit. How great is our God! We have no lack in Him-only potential!

God You Said....
- While the earth remains, seedtime and harvest, cold and heat, winter and summer, and day and night shall not cease. *(Genesis 8:22)*

God Established the Principle of Seedtime and Harvest
When God created the first living thing, He gave it the ability to grow and multiply. How? Through the Seed. Your Entrepreneurial life began by the seed principle. Every act of your life since your birth has operated by the seed principle – springing from good seeds or bad seeds you have sown – whether or not you were consciously aware of your seed planting. The principle continues today. To overcome life's problems, reach your potential in life, see your life become fruitful, multiplied, replenished (that is, in health, finance, spiritual renewal, family, or your entire being), determine to follow God's law of seedtime and harvest. Sow the seed of His promise in the soil of your need.

God You Said....
- Command those who are rich in this present age not to be haughty, not to trust in uncertain riches but in the living God, who gives us richly all things to enjoy. *(1 Timothy 6:17)*

Riches Are a Responsibility
This verse avoids much misunderstanding about the acquisition or possession of material goods. Paul tells us not to trust in uncertain riches. Here, the word "trust" means "to expect" or "to hope for." We are not to hope for riches or expect them to bring us security

or deliverance. Why does the writer tell us security or deliverance? Why does he tell us that? Because riches are so transient. Values change, and earthly riches are only as good as the present value. What is valuable today might not be valuable tomorrow; thus the wisdom of our trusting is—putting our hope—in God alone to make provision for us. Further, we must never let the presence of wealth make us think that we are better than others or that we can be irresponsible or indulgent. It is a responsibility, a great responsibility, to have great wealth; and the Christian Entrepreneur must always remember that much is required of those to whom much is given.

God You Said….

- Beloved, I pray that you may prosper in all things and be in health, just as your soul prospers. *(3 John 2)*

Prosperity Is a Result

It is clear that God wants His children to prosper. How can anyone deny that? However, prosperity should not be the end in itself. It ought to be the result of a quality of life, commitment, dedication, and action that is in line with God's Word. In this text the word "prosper" literally means "to help on the road" or "succeed in reaching." It clearly implies that divine prosperity is not a momentary, passing phenomenon, but rather it is an ongoing, progressing state of success and well-being. It is intended for every area of our lives; the spiritual, the physical, the emotional, and the material. However, God does not want us to unduly emphasize any one area. The Christian Entrepreneur must maintain a balance.

God You Said….

- No one can serve two masters; for either he will hate the one and love the other, or else he will be loyal to the one and despise the other. You cannot serve God and mammon. (*Matthew 6:24*)

Choosing God or Money

The issue of money is mentioned frequently in the Bible because money can be a most insidious, beguiling, and pervasive temptation. Here in Matthew 6:24, Jesus teaches that the problem with wealth or riches ("mammon") is that we become mastered by it when we choose to serve mammon instead of God. The word "serve" used here means "to be enslaved to." Our choice of masters is not solely an issue of advisability (a choice of priorities), nor is it a mere question of accountability (a moral choice). Rather, it is a clear issue of impossibility (no choice). The Christian Entrepreneur simply must choose between serving God and serving mammon. To serve God fully means to have money issues under control.

God You Said....

• Honor the Lord with your possessions, and with the first fruits of all your increase; so your barns will be filled with plenty, and your vats will overflow with new wine. (***Proverbs 3:9-10***)

The first fruits refers to the practice of giving to God's use, the first and best portion of the harvest (Deuteronomy 26:9-11). Many people give God their leftovers. If they can afford to donate anything, they do so. These people may be sincere and contribute willingly, but their attitude is nonetheless backwards. It is better to give God the first part of our income. This demonstrates that God, not possessions, has first place in our lives and that our resources belong to Him (we are only managers of God's resources). Giving to God first helps us conquer greed, helps us properly manage God's resources, and opens us up to receive God's special blessings. Yet these verses should not be taken as a formula for getting rich. They speak of what righteous people can reasonably expect in life, not what God promises to return on investments.

Things To Remember

1. Acknowledge the Positives - you are what you focus on. Pay attention to all the positives in your life each day.

2. Practice Daily Gratitude - begin by practicing gratitude on a daily basis. List mentally or in a journal, five things you are thankful for each day.

3. Draft Your Abundance Statement - if you are ready to take things a step further, write your own abundance statement of twenty words or less.

4. Do not fret.

5. Trust in the Lord.

6. Delight yourself in the Lord.

7. Commit your way to the Lord.

8. Be still before the Lord.

9. Wait on the Lord.

Chapter 9

THE CHRISTIAN ENTREPRENEUR & THE ACHIEVER'S ATTITUDE

It's been my experience that your outward existence will inevitably match what the heart and mind have already decided to do or be. Each of us has an overall pattern of thinking that is either positive or negative. The pattern you choose affects every aspect of your life. First of all, your basic attitude affects your belief in your potential for success, i.e. "Can I run a successful company"? A negative attitude causes the Christian Entrepreneur to doubt their ability to achieve, while belief in their potential makes them willing to take the necessary action for success.

The achiever's attitude will also allow you to view challenges as opportunities rather than threats. Christian Entrepreneurs with negative attitudes think, "I can't..." or "I doubt..." In contrast, each time they act from a positive attitude, their self-confidence is enhanced, their ability to achieve is proven, and they know they can succeed.

Christian Entrepreneurs who have a negative attitude have buried their ability to see opportunities. A positive achiever's attitude opens their eyes to so many opportunities that their challenge becomes which opportunity to choose.

Finally, the Achiever's Attitude gives us the power to become who we want to become, and determines who others think we are. Who you are is not determined by how you look, where you live, or who your parents were. Who you are is a function of specific choices that you have made. You are where you are and what you are because of the dominating thoughts in your mind. After all, as a man "thinks in his heart, so is he" (Proverbs 23:7). We are what we think we are—not what we appear to be on the outside. An absolutely essential ingredient for success is a positive self-image. The world operates on the basis of the law of attraction: what you are and what you think will attract corresponding conditions. If you have a negative self-image, you attract negative results. If your self-image is positive, you attract positive results. This may appear simplistic, but it is absolutely true. Your mental picture of yourself determines the measure of confidence you bring to using your potential and working toward your goals. Psychologists estimate we use less than a third of our actual potential. By increasing your potential even slightly, you can make a sizable improvement in your effectiveness.

God You Said....

Have I not commanded you? Be strong and of good courage; do not be afraid nor be dismayed, for the Lord your God is with you wherever you go. *(Joshua 1:9)*

Christian Entrepreneurs are to encourage themselves with the promises and presence of God. They cannot let the sense of their own infirmities dishearten them; God is all-sufficient. God has commanded, called, and commissioned the Christian Entrepreneur to run a successful business, along with changing and ruling the marketplace. They can be sure that God will walk it out with them. The Christian Entrepreneur also has to understand that God will never leave them nor forsake them in their efforts.

God You Said....

- And we know that all things work together for good to those who love God, to those who are the called according to His purpose. *(Romans 8:28)*

The Christian Entrepreneur is under God's providence, all things, even their sorrows, trials and persecutions, work together for the blessing. This precious assurance is not to all mankind, saint and sinner, but is limited to a class of Christian Entrepreneurs. To them that love God. The love of God is the very foundation of the

Christian Entrepreneurs life. The Christian Entrepreneur who has been called by God, has accepted the call to start and run a Godly business. Many others are called, but only those who hear and obey are chosen. The evidence that we are the called is that we love God and this call was purposed from the time that God promised a Deliverer of the fallen race.

God You Said....

- But you, be strong and do not let your hands be weak, for your work shall be rewarded. (*2 Chronicles 15:7*)

Azariah encouraged the men of Judah to keep up the good work, "For your work shall be rewarded." This is an inspiration for the Christian Entrepreneur too. Recognition and reward are great motivators that have two dimensions: (1). The temporal dimension, living by God's standards may result in acclaim here on earth. (2). The eternal dimension, permanent recognition and reward will be given in the next life. Don't be discouraged if you feel your faith in God is going unrewarded here on earth. The best rewards are not in this life, but in the life to come. Be strong and do not let your hands be weak.

God You Said....

- If you can believe, all things are possible to him who believes. (*Mark 9:23*)

Jesus words do not mean that we can automatically obtain anything we want if we just think positively. Jesus meant that anything is possible if we believe, because nothing is too difficult for God. We cannot have everything we pray for as if by magic; but with faith, we can have everything we need to serve him and get our task done while here on earth. This scripture is a challenge to our faith. There is no question that Jesus can do all things. The only question is whether we can or will trust him. The Christian Entrepreneurs desires must be in accord with God's will.

God You Said....

- What then shall we say to these things? If God is for us, who can be against us? (**Romans 8:31**)

The word "things" refer to God's purpose. If God has done everything from foreknowledge to glorification for us, all adversaries are powerless. Paul asserts that God is for us and therefore no one can succeed against us. No one, means no one. Your business is destined to succeed if you remain faithful to it.

God You Said....

- I can do all things through Christ who strengthens me. (**Philippians 4:13**)

It is important to note that the emphasis is not so much on achievement as it is on willingness to allow Christ's power to sustain you in difficulty and scarcity, and to enhance the enjoyment of abundance and prosperity. Such faith is a stimulant to believe for all Christ's sufficiency in facing all your business issues. Believe that when God asks you to do something, He is able to provide the strength you need to do it.

God You Said....

- That you do not become sluggish, but imitate those who through faith and patience inherit the promises. (**Hebrews 6:12**)

The Christian Entrepreneur is encouraged not to become sluggish, which is translated as dull, lazy, and slothful, but must go forward constantly for their own good with patience, less anyone should object and say that these things are impossible to do. The Christian Entrepreneur is also encouraged to consider the examples of their ancestors and follow them, these are the likes of the Abraham's, the Joseph's, the Stephen's and the Rahab's to name a few. The Christian Entrepreneur must keep in mind that faith and patience, which are the key qualities essential to steadfastness, must be found in those who inherit the promises. The Christian Entrepreneur who always keeps the end in view, will not become slothful. Hope is the means of ensuring this.

God You Said....

- Yet in all these things we are more than conquerors through Him who loved us. (***Romans 8:37***)

The Christian Entrepreneur is already victorious in their businesses. The Apostle Paul said that we are more than conquerors through Him who loved us, this means that we are so far from being conquered by our circumstances, setbacks and disappointments because of the love of Christ. We have been designed to rule, dominant and take over the marketplace. Matthew 5:16 teaches that "we should let our light so shine before men, that they may see our good works and glorify our Father in heaven."

God You Said....

- You are of God, little children, and have overcome them, because He who is in you is greater than he who is in the world. (*1 John 4:4*)

By the illumination of the Holy Spirit, who is greater than the enemy, the Christian Entrepreneur can overcome any and all setbacks regarding their business, not through unchristian worldly sources, but through the word of God.

God You Said....

- Being confident of this very thing, that He who has begun a good work in you will complete it until the day of Jesus Christ. (*Philippians 1:6*)

The Christian Entrepreneur can be confident that they will maintain their fruitful activity or fruitful business until Christ returns. They can base their belief, not on their own faithfulness, but on God's purpose and faithfulness until Christ returns. Believe with confidence that God will accomplish the good work He started in you.

God You Said....

- The race is not to the swift, nor the battle to the strong, nor bread to the wise, nor riches to men of understanding, nor favor to men of skill; but time and chance happen to them all. (***Ecclesiastes 9:11***)

The fastest runner doesn't always win the race, and the strongest warrior doesn't always win the battle. The wise sometimes go hungry, and the skillful are not necessarily wealthy. And those who are educated don't always lead successful lives. It is all decided by chance, by being in the right place at the right time. Time and chance happen to them all. A sovereign Providence breaks men's measures, and blasts their hopes, and teaches them that the way of man is not in himself, but subject to the divine will of God. We must use means, but not trust in them; if we succeed, we must give God the praise (Psalm 44:3); but if we are crossed, the Christian Entrepreneur must acquiesce in His will and take their lot.

<u>Things to Remember:</u>

1. Clearly decide on what it is that you desire — be precise, write down details.

2. Use your imagination and consistently visualize the results you want.

3. Truly believe in your pursuit, no matter how many obstacles appear.

4. Enthusiastically take action and doggedly overcome challenges.

5. Be positive, expect the results you want.

Chapter 10

THE CHRISTIAN ENTREPRENEUR & MONEY

The Bible says "set not your heart upon riches when they increase." No man is forbidden to make money, but men are taught continually what to do with the money they do make.

Christian Entrepreneurs who want to get rich, fall into various temptations and are trapped. They also fall into many foolish and harmful desires that plunge men into ruin and destruction. For the love of money is a root of all kinds of evil. Some people, eager for money, have wandered from the faith and pierced themselves with many sorrows (1 Timothy 6:9-10).

The Bible teaches that those who have money should devote it to the service of God. God gives man the power to get wealth, and they are to seek His glory in all their money getting. This will turn places of business into sanctuaries. Mark the words, "Honor the Lord with thy substance," with what you have on hand, and then ever afterward with "the first-fruits of all thine increase." How many give no more to God's cause after their income is doubled, or even tripled, than they did before! They keep to the miserable paltry dollar standard, though they could give $20.00 now as easily as they use to give $1.00. Honor God with the increase.

The Bible teaches that ten per cent of the money that comes into our possession is His, and that the man who withholds that portion is robbing God. This is the most searching word the Bible has to say on the money question, and should not be lightly passed over by any Christian Entrepreneur who claims to be redeemed by the precious blood of Christ. "And all the tithe of the land, whether of the seed of the land, or of the fruits of the tree, is the Lord's."

Dear Christian Entrepreneur, are you using the money that has come into your possession according to the teaching of God's Word? Are you honoring God with it by presenting to Him not less than one tenth of all your income? If not, prove God herewith and see if he will not be as good as His Word in Proverbs 3:9, 10 and Malachi 3:10.

God You Said…..
- A feast is made for laughter, and wine makes merry; but money answers everything. *(Ecclesiastes 10:19)*

The preacher has just stated the purpose of the feast (laughter) and wine (makes merry). Money, on the other hand, can be spent or invested and the one who has it always retains options that are automatically forfeited by the person who has spent all his cash.

The Christian Entrepreneur cannot be afraid of money, because money answers all things. The Christian Entrepreneur will need money to buy inventory, buy buildings, rent a space, buy trucks, pay bills, pay employees, etc.

As Christian business people, we have to understand that money management is going to play a key role in the success of our business and the one that does not manage their money will forfeit their options.

God You Said….
- No servant can serve two masters; for either he will hate the one and love the other, or else he will be loyal to the one and despise the other. You cannot serve God and mammon. (*Luke 16:13)*

The Christian Entrepreneurs attitude towards money is indicative of one's submission to or rebellion against God's Lordship.

The Christian Entrepreneur must be loyal to God and forsake any ambition that compromises his or her commitment to Him.

God You Said....

- The generous soul will be made rich, and he who waters will also be watered himself. *(Proverbs 11:25)*

All good comes from God alone (James 1:17), and He gives such an all-sufficiency that we need never suffer any loss (2 Corinthians 9:7-10). Many are afraid to trust Him with their all, and He certainly tests us, even asking us to trust Him down to the last handful of meal in the barrel (1 Kings 17:10-16). Here again is the divine law of sowing and reaping. We are to be liberal in benevolence, not in doctrine. Generosity prospers a person, stinginess impoverishes.

God You Said....

- The rich rules over the poor, and the borrower is servant to the lender. *(Proverbs 22:7)*

Our hearts, our feelings of love and desire dictates to a great extent how we live, because we always fine time to do what we enjoy. Solomon tells us to guard our heart above all else, making sure we concentrate on those desires that will keep us on the right path. Make sure your affections push you in the right direction. Put boundaries on your desires; don't go after everything you see. Look straight ahead, keep your eyes fixed on your goal, and don't get sidetracked on detours that lead to disappointment and setbacks.

God You Said....

- Wealth and riches will be in his house, and his righteousness endures forever. *(Psalm 112:3)*

The godly will have abundance and contentment, because their heart is satisfied in God alone. Often when gold comes in, the gospel goes out; but it is not so with the blessed man. Prosperity does not destroy the holiness of his life, or the humility of his heart. His character stands the test of examination, overcomes the temptations of wealth, survives the assaults of slander, outlives the afflictions of time, and endures the trial of the last great day. The righteousness of a true saint endureth for ever, because it springs from the same root as the righteousness of God, and is, indeed, the reflection of it. So long as the Lord abideth righteous, He will maintain by His grace the righteousness of His people.

God You Said....

- While the earth remains, seedtime and harvest, cold and heat, winter and summer, and day and night shall not cease. *(Genesis 8:22)*

While the earth remains, and man upon it, there shall be summer and winter. It is plain that this earth is not to remain always. It, and all the works in it, must shortly be burned up; and we look for new heavens and a new earth, when all these things shall be dissolved. But as long as it does remain, God's providence will cause the course of times and seasons to go on, and make each to know its place. And on this word the Christian Entrepreneur depends, that thus it shall be. We see God's promises to the creatures made good, and may infer that His promises to all believers shall be so.

God You Said....

- That I may cause those who love me to inherit wealth, that I may fill their treasuries. (*Proverbs 8:21*)

Spiritual and eternal things are the only real and substantial things. Worldly possessions and riches are but shadows that are here today and gone tomorrow, but spiritual blessings, though seen only by the eye of faith, are the real substances, for they have God's own power operating in them. Note that not only does the Lord promise substance (wealth) to the Christian Entrepreneur, but He promises to "fill" their treasuries also.

God You Said....

- No one can serve two masters. Either he will hate the one and love the other, or he will be devoted to the one and despise the other. You cannot serve both God and Money. (*Matthew 6:24*)

The issue of money is mentioned frequently in the Bible because money can be a most insidious, beguiling, and pervasive temptation (1 Timothy 6:10). Here in Matthew 6:24, Jesus teaches that the problem with wealth or riches ("mammon") is that we become mastered by it when we choose to serve mammon instead of God. The word "serve" used here means "to be enslaved to." Our choice of masters is not solely an issue of advisability (a choice of priorities), nor is it a mere question of accountability (a moral choice). Rather, it is a clear issue of impossibility (no choice). One simply must choose between serving God and serving mammon. To serve God fully means to have money issues under control.

God You Said....

- Then Jesus said to His disciples, Assuredly, I say to you that it is hard for a rich man to enter the kingdom of heaven. And again I say to you, it is easier for a camel to go through the eye of a needle than for a rich man to enter the kingdom of God. *(Matthew 19:23-24)*

Jesus uses an exaggeration to teach that it is impossible for one who trust in riches over God to enter heaven. The key point for the Christian Entrepreneur, however, is to be reminded about the dangers of wealth and possessions. They can become our God, our stumbling block, our choking point, our diversion, and our downfall if they become the thing we cannot give up to follow Jesus.

God You Said....

- Jesus said to him, "If you want to be perfect, go, sell what you have and give to the poor, and you will have treasure in heaven; and come, follow Me." *(Matthew 19:21)*

Jesus issues a stern challenge designed to show the man that he has not observed the spirit of the commandments, in spite of his claim. In fact, his selfish attitude in making an idol of wealth reveals that he had broken the very first Commandment, Exodus 20:3 "You shall have no other gods before Me."

God You Said....

- He who gives to the poor will lack nothing, but he who closes his eyes to them receives many curses. *(Proverbs 28:27)*

God pronounces a blessing of benevolence to the poor, for such resembles His own benevolence. Jesus taught that good deeds shall be rewarded with good, (Luke 6:38). The covetous man, however, closes his eyes to others' needs, and while he may pray "God bless you," he will not be God's instrument to bless. The Christian Entrepreneur should always have a spirit of giving.

God You Said....

- But those who desire to get rich fall into temptation and a snare and into many foolish and harmful desires that plunge men into ruin and destruction. For the love of money is a root of all kinds of evil, for which some strayed from the faith in their greediness, and pierced themselves through with many sorrows. *(1 Timothy 6:9-10)*

A restless desire to be rich subjects one to great spiritual peril. Loving money opens our lives to the ultimate deception, because the heart of the issue is lordship, a person cannot serve both God and money. We are instead to purse true riches which are spiritual in nature; righteousness, godliness, faith, love patience, and gentleness. Job declared that if he put his trust in money, it would mean he had denied God in heaven (Job 31:24-28).

God You Said....

- Command those who are rich in this present age not to be haughty, nor to trust in uncertain riches but in the living God, who gives us richly all things to enjoy. Let them do good, that they be rich in good works, ready to give, willing to share, storing up for themselves a good foundation for the time to come, that they may lay hold on eternal life. *(I Timothy 6:17-19)*

The passage avoids much misunderstanding about the acquisition or possession of material goods. Paul tells the Christian Entrepreneur not to trust in uncertain riches. Here, the word "trust" means "to expect" or "to hope for." The Christian Entrepreneur is not to hope for riches or expect them to bring them security or deliverance. The reason being is because riches are transient. Values change, and earthly riches are only as good as their present value. What is valuable today might not be valuable tomorrow; thus the wisdom of our trusting - putting our hope - in God alone to make provision for us. Further, the Christian Entrepreneur must never let the presence of wealth make them think that they are better than others or that they can be irresponsible or indulgent. It is a responsibility, a great responsibility, to have great wealth; and the Christian Entrepreneur must always remember that much is required of those to whom much is given.

God You Said....

- A faithful man will abound with blessings, but he who hastens to be rich will not go unpunished. *(Proverbs 28:20)*

Faithfulness, whether to God or to men will be rewarded, and so this is the way of blessings, for even if men do not reward the man who is faithful, yet the Lord will. "Mammon" was the personification of riches, (Matthew 6:24; Luke 16:9), and many people make an idol of it. When man hastily, or in a short time, becomes rich, though he cannot be directly charged with fraud and injustice, yet he is not innocent in the minds of men, or free from their suspicions and jealousies of him. A man that makes haste to be rich is opposed to him that is faithful and true to his word and contracts.

God You Said....

- Do not overwork to be rich; because of your own understanding, cease! Will you set your eyes on that which is not? For riches certainly make themselves wings; they fly away like an eagle toward heaven. *(Proverbs 23:4-5)*

Wisdom here no doubt has to do with human wisdom that is put out in an endeavor to gain worldly riches. God's command is that all men be content with having a sufficiency of life's needs. Sometimes God gives much more than we need so that our abundance may be a means of helping others, (2 Corinthians 8:13-15; 9:8-11). Superior abundance ought not to be squandered. But mere riches for riches' sake is not to be sought. Nothing is more certain than that man cannot possess worldly riches for any great length of time. If riches are not taken away from man, man is eventually taken away from them by death. This verse finds a N.T. echo in 1 John 2:15-17. These "are not" in that they are so very temporary, and then they fly away through theft, inflation, taxation, poor management, etc. (1 Timothy 6:17-19).

God You Said....
- He who loves silver will not be satisfied with silver; nor he who loves abundance, with increase. This also is vanity. *(Ecclesiastes 5:10)*

The Christian Entrepreneur must recognize that no amount of silver or increasing abundance will ever satisfy the human soul. We are uniquely created to worship God alone; nothing else can truly bring lasting peace and satisfaction.

God You Said....
- A good name is to be chosen rather that great riches, loving favor rather than silver and gold. *(Proverbs 22:1)*

A good name is not just *reputation*, which may not truly fit the man, but is rather *character*, which is what he really is. A bad man may maintain a good reputation for a time, but eventually, his real character will be known. Character is better than riches, because its foundation is better, its acquisition harder, its compass wider, its utility greater, its duration longer, its loss more fatal. God will be the Friend of a man in whose spirit there is no guile.

God You Said....
- Now in my prosperity I said, I shall never be moved. *(Psalm 30:6)*

This is the confession in which David acknowledges that he had been justly and deservedly punished for his foolish and rash security, in forgetting his mortal and mutable condition as a man, and in setting his heart too much on prosperity. Here David is saying when fortune smiled upon me on every side, and no danger appeared to occasion fear, my mind sunk as it were into a deep sleep, and

I flattered myself that my happy condition would continue, and that things would always go on in the same course. This carnal confidence frequently creeps upon the Christian Entrepreneur when they indulge themselves in their prosperity. By this we are taught to be on our guard when in prosperity, that Satan may not bewitch us with his flatteries. The more bountifully God deals with any one, the more carefully ought he to watch against such snares. It is not, indeed, probable that David had become so hardened as to despise God and defy all misfortunes, like many of the great men of this world, who, when immersed among their luxuries, insolently scoff at all God's judgments; but an effeminate listlessness having come over his mind, he became more lukewarm in prayer, nor did he depend on the favor of God; in short, he put too much confidence in his uncertain and transitory prosperity. The Christian Entrepreneur has to be on guard at all times, prosperity will come, but do not set your mind on it.

God You Said....

- Keep your lives free from the love of money and be content with what you have. For He Himself has said, "I will never leave you nor forsake you." *(Hebrews 13:5)*

The author is writing about being covetous, meaning that we want more for ourselves—things that others seem to have and we do not. So he writes, "Be content with what you have. Don't get all riled up about it." It is very interesting that he says, "Be content," and then, "God has told you He will never leave you nor forsake you." When we are discontent and dissatisfied, one of the first thoughts that we normally have is that God has abandoned us, that He does not care about us, that He has not blessed us. Paul says, "Don't think that way." The Christian Entrepreneur has to be content with where they are because God has *not* left them. He will never leave you nor forsake you. You are exactly where He wants you, so you have no reason to be discontent. God has placed you in the body where it pleases Him. And that should be enough for us.

God You Said....

• Getting treasures by a lying tongue is the fleeting fantasy of those who seek death. (***Proverbs 21:6***)

Some people are so hasty to gain material wealth that they are unscrupulous as to how they do so, and so they resort to misrepresentation and fraud in business. But so far from this getting them treasures, it only brings death to them. "Vanity" means a vapor and so it suggests the emptiness of ill-gotten gain, and so there is not the satisfaction expected in that which is not gotten by honest and honorable means. They probably do not realize that they are seeking death, but this shall be their end.

God You Said....

• Now Godliness with contentment is great gain. For we brought nothing into this world, and it is certain we can carry nothing out. (***1 Timothy 6:6-8***)

The Christian Entrepreneurs contentment does not come from how much money they have, but from the freedom that results from understanding that they are living in God's provision.

God You Said....

• Honor the Lord with your possessions, and with the first-fruits of all your increase; so your barns will be filled with plenty, and your vats will overflow with new wine. (***Proverbs 3:9-10***)

The Christian Entrepreneur is expected to have an offering in their hands when they come to worship the Lord. In the Old Testament days, it was not possible to worship the Lord rightly with empty hands; so too we today are to worship and honor Him with our substance, by bringing the tithes and offerings. We live upon annual products to keep us in constant dependence on God. God, who is the first and best, must have the first and best of everything. To honor the Lord with the first-fruits is to acknowledge His ownership of all things; to refuse to do so is to deny His ownership of all things. He blesses those who honor Him.

spirit constantly traveling with me through the jungles of this life is continuing to sing to my patients and families as part of my chaplain's ministry at the hospital or with the hospice. The comfort this brings to them reminds me of my mother telling me that if I focus on the comfort of those hurting, dying and grieving, God will take care of my own grief, pain and struggles in life. This became so real for me after a major back surgery that tremendously slowed me down and really challenged me as I walked around the hospital ministering to patients, families and staff. The more I yearned to be used of God to comfort and encourage those that were grieving, the less I thought about my own pain.

Grieving the Loss of a Sibling:

When you lose a sibling you lose you oldest playmate.

Every loss we experience in our lives leaves a gaping hole. However, the death of a sibling creates an especially tender void. Our siblings are the closest part of our childhood history. Our siblings might even know some very important secrets about us that nobody else knows, not even our parents. They are our very first and closest playmates. A sibling may be the only person we fight with but when someone else tries to get in between, both siblings forget their own disagreements and gang up to fight the "intruder" in defending their sibling. The death of a sibling therefore casts an unusual shadow on our future and their absence from our lives is devastating in its own way.

Our siblings form the very first peer group and so their death remind us of our own mortality, especially when you lose a younger sibling. Siblings play a very important role in our family of origin even after we are grown up. Together, the siblings share the responsibilities of caring for other siblings, younger or older, especially for those that are disadvantaged or challenged by one thing or the other. They share the care

71

of elderly parents. In every family, each sibling has their own unique role in all that happens among them. So when one dies, there is a very definite disruption of life among the surviving siblings and the parents if still alive. If the dead sibling had his/her own family, under normal circumstances, the surviving siblings are expected to take the added responsibilities to watch over his/her family to a certain extent, especially if there are young children. They leave a gap in the caring of their parents if they are still alive which must now be shared between the surviving siblings.

In every family, there are games, jokes, hobbies, and holiday activities unique to the siblings. So the absence of any of them will inevitably affect the rest. As we grieve the loss of our siblings, especially the younger ones, when our parents are still alive, there may be some form of guilt and wishing that you should be the one who died. The devastation and crushing pain of losing a child is the worst to be endured by any parent.

This is the worst blow to watch your own parents battling such grief and you really don't know how to comfort them. At times you are even ashamed to grieve your loss, even though it is real and necessary, around your parents knowing what they are going through. You end up suppressing it and getting so engrossed with other people's grief to the point of neglecting the need to heal your own grief too. Be sure to acknowledge and process it like everyone else. Give yourself time and space to do this. Take time and do whatever comforts you best to remember your sibling. Find the time and place to talk about him/her with your family or friends. Eulogize your sibling if you feel strong enough to do so. Write a farewell letter and tell him anything you wish you had told them before they passed away.

In some instances, sibling rivalry may have left some bitter feelings that were not quite solved before one of them dies. Despite any disagreements, love and affection may still co-exist with rivalry and jealousy. The surviving sibling may experience guilt for the unresolved issues or their inability to care for or protect the one who died. These may be normal feelings which could also be coupled with wishful thinking. The reality is that there is nothing one can do to reverse the clock of life. The best the grieving person can do is to use this as a motivation for positive change in how they treat those still alive around them. One needs to go a step further, forgive oneself and move on as best as humanly possible. Find a way of doing something in memory of your deceased sibling. Support the family they left behind and this will help put some meaning into the relationship that is now gone for ever.

I lost 2 younger brothers, both at their prime age of 40, which left a deep pain in me for many years. I often asked God why He would take them, both leaving very young children, instead of taking me whose children were older. Through my grief, God reminded me of all the concern both my brothers had for me, always challenging me to take good care of me, their elder sister. They had both constantly expressed deep faith in me, one to the extent of telling me that he knew his family would be taken good care of as long as I was there. This was actually long before he died in an accident.

As a result of this, I took it upon myself to do everything I could to care of me and with my other siblings also help educate the nephews and nieces they left behind. This did not mean me forgetting them but doing something to honor them. The surviving sibling(s) might also devise a plan or project in honor of their departed sibling and keep their memory alive. Some options would include making a family scrap book with pictures and stories of the deceased sibling. Highlight their adult life, achievements and the family of their own if any. A foundation in their honor can also be established or money donated to charity that might have interested them during their lifetime. Another way of sustaining their legacy if they left a family behind is working with the surviving spouse and their children to decide what they would want to do in this respect. They might want to do an annual event around the death anniversary in their memory. You can join in such a venture and help to achieve that wish. As you all do this and encourage the support of other family members, you will all be able to process your grief and healing in a meaningful way for all.

The most important thing that the death of a sibling reminds us is our own mortality again. Whether the deceased sibling is younger or older than us, they are still in your generation and that means death can catch up you at any time just as it did with them. As the journey of grief continues, one must get to a point in their loss of whatever kind, when they must choose life and the need to reconstruct their lives beyond their loss. While life without your loved one will never be the same again for you, you can control the way you change – for better or for worse. One will need to choose what is good and necessary to carry over from the past into the future.

Inevitably, something will have to be done away with in order to reconstruct one's life. Out of the new necessities of one's new life and new identity beyond the loss, there may be a need to develop new skills or characteristics. There will be moments of fear, guilt or apprehension, doubting whether you need to or can even move on after all the pain you feel today. Thank God for the hope that faith brings is us for such crossroads of life. Unfortunately, the pain of grief and loss is one experience each of us must some day undergo at one time or another. There is a motivational speaker, Les Brown, who says that if the messenger of doom has not visited with you, he may be knocking at your door in a little while or in the future. It is therefore important that we support those that are grieving today because tomorrow may be our turn.

Grieving the Loss of Broken Relationships

As we grow from one stage of life to the next; from childhood to adolescence; adolescence to young adulthood and finally into our fading declining stage, we develop all kinds of relationships. There are those we played with during our developing years, experimenting on anything and everything that captured our imagination. There will be those who have been there in different seasons of life, stayed beside us when we were celebrating and enjoying a good life. Then there are those who left and abandoned us when things changed for the worse. And finally there are those that kept vigil beside us when our lives were crashed and almost destroyed by one tragedy or another, like death in a family, getting caught up with criminal events and jail terms. There are those who keep in touch after circumstances cause us to move away from one location to another looking for greener pastures that never materialized.

Among those relationships, some will develop into intimate friendships – our best friends who know almost everything about us. We develop a deep sense of trust and confidence in them that we are occasionally able even to process our thoughts, dreams and aspirations openly with them, knowing that they accept us for who we are, loving us unconditionally. Some of these friendships eventually pave a way for courtship and future marriage. We even get our mutual families involved slowly, blissfully trusting things to keep moving to the right direction.

One party in these relationships might maintain dual relationships outside of the original setup. For one reason or another, they break lose and chose to move on, to the utter shock of the other person who all along never saw it coming and busy planning for a bigger future. Perhaps they were even engaged and way deep into wedding arrangements. The jilted lover gets caught up in total disbelief and denial while the other person moves fast and far away.

This happens often and the damage to the abandoned person can have long lasting damage, at times totally incapacitating the wounded one to such an extent that they can never trust anyone else in the future. Some such people who had started visualizing themselves in a marriage with the other person, have been known shut themselves off to marriage for the rest of their lives. Some develop a very permanent and negative dislike for the opposite sex, even within their families. Some however, gradually recover from the shock, but in a hurry to make it up to themselves might end up hooking themselves urgently just to anyone who comes along, without finding out if they are compatible. Some carry the blame of the broken relationships so heavily and unknowingly expose themselves to future abuse as they do anything to earn the love of whoever comes into their lives next.

Broken relationships have also been known to exist between parents and children. Where children have been sexually molested or abused by parents or other relatives, a permanent damage takes place to the extent that when they grow up and leave home they want nothing to do with their abusive parents ever again. I have had painful encounters with lonely patients who when asked if their parents have visited them will say they have had no contact with them for many years since they left home. I vividly remember a young woman in her early twenties, admitted with exhaustion and fatigue because of working double shifts for years. Alone and struggling to make a better life for herself, working and schooling, she just crashed. She had no idea where her parents were for the last seven years since she left home, living with boyfriends, finally hoping to marry her current one. She had no contact with her siblings either because her brothers also sexually abused her together with their father. I felt a sense of deep pain and desperation in her heart trying to survive alone and wanting nothing to do with her family of origin. This was too painful to comprehend and imagine what goes on in her mind when she breaks up with any of her boyfriends who might also just misuse her knowing she has no one else to turn to or even to protect her.

Looking at all this and aware that there are many other forms of broken relationships, I am quickly comforted by the remembrance that the one relationship that is secure, unconditional and free is our relationship with God our creator, Jesus our Savior and Holy Spirit our Comforter. The only time that this relationship is broken is when we turn away, look to and trust other men and women for our help and walk away from God. Having gone through a painful divorce myself after 30 years of marriage, I can empathize with anyone struggling and healing from a broken relationship. In my life, I did everything I could or knew how to save my marriage but had to painfully face the reality that even after giving it the best part of my life, my youth and my best intellect, it was not working for me. At that point, it was my long time relationship with Christ and the support of my family of origin, my own children and a few faithful Christian prayerful friends who helped me keep looking up to God for His sustaining grace through a very painful phase of my life.

The impact of broken relationships can be so devastating that some people never recover from it but end up in self destructive habits like alcohol, drugs and substance abuse and dependency in an effort to soothe their heartache. It matters how well grounded one is in their faith and who the cornerstone of their survival in life is. Paul said that while we may be crashed and tortured from all sides, yet if we remain in Christ we are not totally destroyed.

The Loss of Physical Ability

For as long as one is healthy, agile and able to do all the normal things that are relevant to one's age, desire and ability, it is hard to imagine the kind and depth of grief experienced by people when all the above is suddenly or gradually taken away either by illness, accidents or even mental conditions that steal the will to live and perform. At the peak of one's life, we take so much for granted that we can run, walk, sit or stand, sleep, eat, drink and swallow automatically. The fact that we can even blink, open or close our eyes as we choose without even giving it a thought, is actually a miracle.

But as you look around you in the community, in your family, at church, in your place of work or wherever else you interact with people, you start to notice people who are incapacitated in many ways. They face all kinds of challenges and can barely perform most of the things you do for yourself and others automatically. If you are anywhere in the medical field, in hospitals in any of the many disciplines that are involved in patient care of one kind or another, you will begin to notice and appreciate many of the very minute or simple things that the sick can no longer do on their own. Some are on ventilators and tubes of all kinds that are either breathing for them or literary sustaining their lives. How many times do we stop to thank God that we can breath the God-given fresh air, see the beauty of His creation, smell the roses and everything good, feel the taste of what we are eating or drinking, be able to void on our own and do a million and one things that millions can not do?

Diseases like cancer of the throat make it very hard to swallow, colon cancer results in all kinds of complications and some people end up with colostomy bag through which they void, some for the rest of their lives. Others have tubes inserted in their throat and can no longer speak audibly like you and me. Many have lost different limbs and other organs in accidents or major illnesses and have to be fitted with artificial limbs as a result of which their physical activities are greatly reduced or altered. There are numerous other changes in people's lives for me to list in this document.

As I reflect on all the above, and from my interactions with people in many of these categories, I cannot even start to imagine or describe the grief that must accompany most of these experiences by people who have been able bodied and very active in their lives. Some must now depend on family and friends for survival. Others end up in mental institutions and other medical facilities where they can be cared for. I have listened to the saddest and heart rending stories from many patients who wish their lives could turn around even a little. I have gotten to a point in life when I am conscious of how blessed I am that I can swallow food and water as I desire. Having been completely grounded and bed-ridden for months after a major back surgery, I thank God every waking moment, and remember to pray for those that have to live under such conditions for much longer. I am constantly reminding myself and others never to take anything for granted because the absence of these abilities has resulted in great grief for millions of people.

As a chronic pain advocate, I am aware of those that can no longer take care of their families as a result of these debilitating aches and pains, especially when they are ridiculed as just fussing or being too sensitive to pain. I know the deep grief of a father whose life has been totally altered by an incapacitating back pain that means he can no longer play soccer or any games with a teenage son he and his wife prayed for, for over ten years. This and many other parents in his boat will do or give anything in life to be able to play or do even the simplest things with their children. Yet those who can are not even aware of these gifts.

There are millions of couples who grieve throughout their lives that for one reason or another, they cannot bear children and some are not even physically able to adopt those that have no parents. There are all kinds of physical disabilities endured by millions everywhere that impact people's lives painfully and cause great physical and emotional grief. The sad thing is that often times these people do not get the support and sympathy they deserve to ease their pain. Many a times, we even react ignorantly and hurt them even more.

I had a humbling experience listening to a lady friend of mine who had all her life wanted to get married and have many children of her own. But for many different reasons and broken relationships, she never got married until the age of 54. She narrated many incidents when in the company of her different friends of both gender, she was made to feel less of a woman because she did not have any children. Without knowing her deep desire to have children, some went as far as to assume and tell her that she was too self-centered and did not want children. Unaware of what was going on in her life, a man colleague shared with another man friend that his wife was now expecting a baby and beginning to feel like a "real" woman. My friend wept as she narrated this incident, trying to help me understand the many women out there grieving for unfulfilled dreams. But instead of receiving sympathy and understanding, they felt judged and condemned for reasons beyond their control. Her sadness, and I guess of many others like her, was that many things were usually assumed about them and people were not even bothered to find out why they were who they were, and the fact there may be many unknown and unspoken reasons why they had no children of their own. After that I also remembered a young man who had shared with me the pain of letting go of a girl he had courted and dated for many years, to a point where they were beginning to consider the possibility of marriage. Unfortunately the girl got involved with one of their common friend and became pregnant even though they never got married. This young man, being a strong believer in the sanctity of marriage and God's part in the family, was so determined to pray and wait for a God fearing wife who would do ministry with him in the future, God willing. He too shared the many times people challenged him about his choice to wait or go it slow in the process of looking for a God fearing future wife. In the effort of self preservation and protection from a repeated broken heart, he did not want to rush into a serious relationship to please others, unless he felt comfortable to do so. He too was grieving the loss of his broken relationship, but there being no visible "death' to those around him, he received very little meaningful support and encouragement to believe in the future or sympathy for what he had lost. This continues to show how we as a society, even among believers, are often unduly ignorant of what others might be going through or why they are where or who they are in life. I am more and more sensitized to being less judgmental and assuming, but more tolerant of other people around me.

I also got a rude awakening as I listened to a young man who had battled cancer for over five years from his early teens. He talked of losing all his hair after the chemotherapy treatment for his cancer. For a vibrant young man who had lots of beautiful and healthy hair to style as he wanted, this was a big blow to his image and self esteem.

Ashamed of his bold head, he started wearing base ball caps and different kinds of hats everywhere he went. Without knowing his story, many people made jokes about it. In some places, he was forced to remove his hat before he could be attended to. Initially he would shyly explain why he was wearing the caps or hats but in some cases some people would adamantly tell him that it was not their problem but rules had to be obeyed. He talked of other children, school and classmates laughing at and making dirty jokes at him. He experienced great frustrations because of the many activities he could not participate in due to his sickness and constant body aches and pains. Part or the challenging reality was that cancer was mostly assumed to be a grown-ups disease just like heart, kidney, liver etc diseases. The sad truth is that illnesses do not discriminate between the young and the old but will attack anyone. This meant that most people do not know how to deal with or handle young children and young adults dealing with these diseases. The result is that they end up feeling out of place, neglected or even misunderstood. I know this for a fact because I attend to, counsel and minister at cancer survivors' camps organized by the cancer center at the hospital where I work. The participants range between very young and very senior adults and there are no special guidelines or strategies of catering for the younger ones with issues of self image and chances of their life span being cut short by cancer. This is what causes the isolation and a sense of loneliness for them in many places and situations.

These are just a few illustrations of many other categories of people dealing with equally painful grief but receiving very little sympathy and support most critical for their own healing. I believe it is time we spread word around for everyone to be more sensitive, understanding and caring for people who may appear odd in our midst yet saying nothing about themselves. I see the need for us to be more open to learning from others and being more tolerant and keen to learn why they appear and behave different.

When we think in terms of grief experienced under different situations, then we will be extra careful and considerate, be more prone to offer help as often as we can in order to take away some of their grief. We will remember to emotionally put ourselves in their shoes and think what they may be going through in order to be more innovative and creative in the ways we offer help without making them feel belittled or blamed for their fate. The reality is that what affects us physically has a great deal to do with our emotional and spiritual wellbeing as well. There is an increasing need for those dealing with any physical disability to be given grief support alongside other people undergoing various lose in life.

8

Pastoral Care To The Dying Children And Their Families

One of the most traumatic experiences is when families receive diagnosis of a terminal illness in a child of any age. The devastation results from the fact that we always view children as the best hope and assurance of our future generations. Many would wish they could swap places with the sick child to give them a chance in life. It brings a feeling of family roots being shaken up or pulled out of their very existence. They feel cheated by life and this may result in deep anger and grief.

Having one's child diagnosed with a terminal illness must be the hardest news for any parent or family. In an effort to protect and care for the dying child, people often hide the truth and the details from this child until too late. While this may be seen as a method of care for this child, it often leaves them translating it negatively, especially if they are a little old enough to reason and put two and two together in their experiences. The reality is that they are the ones who are hurting and experiencing all the body changes and decline of various vital organs as the disease advances.

I got exposed to this kind of experience as I walked along with close friends whose only daughter died of cancer at 6 years. This was my little friend Vivian who taught us a great deal through her fight with cancer. I knew this beautiful and happy spirited child from birth and saw her struggle first with diabetes from ages three and a cancer diagnosis a year later. She went through very sickly episodes of chemo and radiation with great support and loving care from both parents who would do practically anything to restore her health. While she loved them back in a very special way and reached out to all her family and friends, she underwent so many drastic changes in her brief journey on earth than any child should ever experience. While nobody wanted to discuss death and dying with or around her, her language, behaviors and interactions with people gradually told us she knew what was happening. She talked a lot about heaven and constantly hugged and assured her parents and friends that she deeply loved them. She gradually started telling her parents that "I *don't belong here and I want to go home*". As her cancer advanced and the effects of chemotherapy and radiation started taking its toll on her, she started distancing herself and would be found in her room quietly crying alone. At times she experienced feelings of loneliness and isolation since she no longer had the strength to play much with her friends or go to school.

Having experienced such statements and reactions from many terminally ill patients during my hospice work or at the critical care units at the hospital, I shared with the parents that she was caringly saying her goodbyes. I suggested to them that they need to emotionally step behind her, listen more keenly and allow her to lead them. She passed away peacefully in her sleep one afternoon less than three weeks thereafter. It was then that the grieving parents would share how finally her language turned into words of farewell with her assuring them she loved Jesus and would be going home with angels to heaven. At one point with many of her family gathered together in one home,

Vivian insisted in anointing everyone present with oil and took offence at those who declined.

The Sunday before she died, Vivian wanted to sing a song and refused help from her mother except that of holding her hand as she sang at her church. This ended up being her farewell to her church family and friends and knowing how sick Vivian was, there was no dry eye at the end of her song.

My little friend Vivian, who had also become like my adopted granddaughter, became a teacher in matters of death and dying to so many of us who walked alongside her in her last days here on earth. She sensitized me and many others of the need to listen and pay attention as the sick children share their innermost feelings which may include the fears of "why me and why now" or other needs. In their care for us and feeling that we are too vulnerable as parents and families to handle their pain and dying, they may not be very direct about it, but may even draw indicative pictures of angels in flight towards heaven, etc like my little friend Vivian did. As pastors and chaplains, we need to help the dying child and family remain open, honest and connected to each other at all times as best as is humanly possible. We can help the family understand the need to help the child remain connected also with her friends and peers to provide some form of continuity and support leveled to her age and mindset. This can be done via video tapes or by inviting their friends home to play simple games as long as the sick child is able and comfortable to do so. This is in line with what I have always found necessary and helpful when dealing with HIV/AIDS patients. Let us work towards *"Adding Life into every day they live"* instead of longing for more days that may never come. Chaplains and the clergy can also mediate between the family and the sick child by keenly listening to both parties and giving spiritual support and the hope of seeing each other again in heaven if either of them should die.

The greatest need is towards the dying moment because while there is every indication that this child is fast declining and dying, it is never easy to let go when the time comes. There may be moments of deep anger, shock and emotional outburst not just against those around, but also against God. Let us avoid comments like *"I understand"*. We really cannot understand another person's grief since grief is very personal and its intensity often dependent on the relationship between the deceased and the grieving person. As much as we know that the grieving person or family are believers comments like *"Your beloved is now in a better place in heaven with God"* may easily hurt a grieving person who was not ready to let go and who may even be angry with the deceased for leaving them alone. I am constantly reminded that some of the words I might say intending to console some grieving person may actually be more hurting than helpful. It is therefore important to be very observant of every reaction from the grieving persons, both verbal and non-verbal. The best one can do is be present and attentive, listen and allow them to express their feelings and emotions. We need to allow them to deal with their grief the way they feel like, without judging them. This may include screaming, rolling themselves on the floor, hitting walls, crying and laughing almost all at the same time Some end up telling jokes or stories about their loved ones even to the extent of what they think the deceased is doing or saying wherever they are at that time after death. The best we can do at such times is being present and attentive to ensure they are safe as they process their grief at that initial stage. At times, being silently present and offering tissue paper, water etc may be the greatest ministry moment than saying unnecessary words that leave heartache than help. After the funeral and the supporting crowds have subsided, continued pastoral visits will be helpful as grief and loss finally hits home with the vivid absence of their child or other loved one. Find out from them how best you can be of help. Drop a sympathy card or other little messages assuring them that you still care and continue to be available for them as best as the Lord leads you, especially if you are their pastor. It is well known that *"Grief Shared helps bond even strangers"*. Your visits or calls will help reduce feelings of loneliness and isolation for the family. It is also very important that while we minister and support the grieving parents, we do not overlook or forget the siblings to the departed child, whether they were younger or older than them. The death will definitely impact their lives in different ways, some of which might never be spoken of or addressed yet they might affect their interpersonal relationships or even school performance. We need to include them and check out how best to help the grieving family. Allow and encourage them to share their feelings of loss and what they need to be able to continue as best as possible. School, classmates, church families and extended families can provide good and much needed support at such times. But allow the children to guide you on how best to help them without imposing everything on them. The same goes for living grandparents who may even be angry at God and everyone as to why their grandchild, their future hope, should die leaving them behind with lives and bodies that are barely functioning. There may also be other close relatives like cousins who grew up with the deceased child or aunties/uncles who were closely involved with his/her growing up and can barely cope with the loss.

9

CHILDREN DEALING WITH
GRIEF & BEREAVEMENT

General statistics have shown that before the age 18 years, one in 20 children will have undergone the loss of one parent. More often than not, the children who lose a parent are at greater risk of depression, withdrawal, struggle with poor self esteem, sexual experimentation, behavior problems, anxiety, etc. These children fall in a category that may require some extra kind of understanding from the family and the community at large. When there is a loss in the family or community, children's grief is often overlooked or disregarded unintentionally. There is great focus on the adults and we often forget that they too are affected and grieving for different reasons, some of which they may never be able to express. The reality is that children grieve even when they do not have the coping mechanisms like adults. They often struggle with sadness, anger, guilt, insecurity and anxiety. The age of every child determines how best they understand death. The preschool ones think death is temporary and the dead loved one will come back later. Those 5 to 9 years of age see death as a separation with their beloved deceased person.

From 9 or 10 years, they slowly begin to understand the finality of death. While they may not fully understand the finality and concept of death and its aftermath, and cannot clearly explain what is going on in their minds, they are equally affected and at a loss like everyone else in the family. Perhaps they are even more deeply impacted by the loss than we may ever know. They may not only be trying to handle and learn to accept the finality of death, but also understand that it is irreversible and dead people function differently from the living. Some may not be at an age of understanding any of the above but are equally confused and frustrated. If proper care and attention is not paid to them during their grieving period, some learn to subdue and hide their feelings and sometimes anger at the dead person who may be a parent, a grandparent, a sibling or a close family member or friend who had a special place in their lives and heart. Many times, these emotions have been known to explode in the most unexpected places and times, even against the wrong people who perhaps had nothing to do with what happened and don't even know anything about it. Unresolved grief can easily manifest itself in people's lives at different stages of life and even be destructive. It is therefore important that while grief and bereavement support is given to the adults in the family, children and young adults are also involved and invited to participate even in the care and eventually funeral arrangements to facilitate for their goodbyes as well as coming to an appropriate closure with the death of their loved one.. Let them freely share their feelings and emotions in an environment that nurtures their healing and coping with death in the future. This also gradually introduces them to their own mortality and encourages them to live meaningful lives. It paves forums of facing and discussing matters of life and death as well as some inevitable crucial stages and crossroads of life that everyone will have to face in the journey of life. Their questions should be kindly and patiently answered and not ridiculed or belittled.

At such moments, children may also be dealing with spiritual issues of where God is in all these issues. Based on what they have heard along the way in adult conversations, some will be heard asking why God would allow the death of their loved ones, especially a parent/grandparent/guardian or a beloved sibling or friend who has meant much to them. As they grow and understand better, feeling embraced and encouraged to grieve in their own way, they become supportive and more accommodating of the grieving adults around them. The hard truth is that death colors every moment of every day for the child when death strikes any family or friend, both at home and school. Adults and parents therefore need to patiently explain and guide them through grief as best as possible in simple clear language.

It is even worse when their emotions and feelings are disregarded, ignored or not acknowledged by those around them. A little later a child may be very angry as reality hits home, as to why a parent would die and leave them alone. Worse still is in the case of an adolescent who will often translate a parent's death as an act of abandonment. They might even blame them for dying of diseases caused by unhealthy habits like cigarette smoking and lung cancer, HIV/AIDS etc. Even in the case of a terminal illness, children might translate it as quitting the battle without considering them.

I had such an encounter with a 17 year old young man brought to the emergency room after an attempted suicide and ending up in one of the critical care units where I was in charge of pastoral care needs. When he was finally revived and stabilized, he was angry with practically everyone who went to his room, demanding that he should have been left to die. I visited him daily, told him I was just checking if he needed help, which he declined, until the fourth day when he burst out in painful tears amidst sobs. I sat quietly with him until he calmed down and was willing to tell me about himself and the attempted suicide. After several days of trying to connect with him, he burst out angrily that his single mother, his only hope and friend, fully aware that nobody else really cared about him should not have died leaving him at the mercy of his very old grandparents who were too old to understand and guide him through his adolescent developmental years. He knew they loved him but they just could not take care of him. He felt they too needed care from someone, but not an added burden of caring for him. He wept and sobbed for a long time and all I could do was sit quietly beside him, praying silently with my hand on his shoulder.

In helping the grieving child, the clergy and pastoral caregivers need to be down to earth with them, be attentive and listen. Children experience lots of different losses in each death of a loved one. In a parent's death, they grieve the loss of their identity, their close friends, familiar living environment when this brings a necessity for them to go live with their grandparents or other relatives. Some start a whole new way of life in foster homes. They need very sensitive support and permission to be themselves in their grief.

There may be periods of poor school performances, bad dreams and nightmares, explosion of bad or violent behaviors confusion about God and heaven etc. Their behaviors may at times be very unpredictable and they need understanding rather than blame and judgment. They need greater compassion, understanding, honesty and love from those around them especially during this critical transition that dramatically affects their lives. The adults also need to be consistent and good in guiding them in their healing process. Good listening and gentle communication helps them to know that grief is natural. Let us not hide away the sorrow, tears and brokenness even as we minister to people, bearing in mind that whatever our roles, we are first and foremost human beings with feelings and emotions like everyone else. This allows others to be natural in their grieving process without striving and struggling to impress us or others around them at these crucial moments.

It is important too, that adults avoid over-shielding children from attending funerals as that deprives them of opportunities to say their good byes, coming to terms with the finality of death and absence of their loved ones from that time forth. Bearing in mind that death is a definite and inevitable part of every human being, it is important that children are taught gradually as they grow in their understanding, etc, what happens at death, funerals or burials. Many people view this negatively, but it is important to induct children into the real matters of life which helps them to handle their grief appropriately even as adults. It also makes it easier for the parents in guiding their children to participate in family grief, embrace whoever has died, tell their stories or even write letters to the deceased as a rite of passage. It also helps the community to see the continuity of life and future even in the loss of a parent or grandparent. It is equally important to offer group support to children under the guidance and close watch of adults and clergy. Watch out too for destructive anger, serious behavior changes, intense withdrawal episodes etc, and address these issues and challenges sensitively, compassionately and without judging them. It may be wise to refer children and families to professional counselors as needs arise. It is increasingly important for people to talk about death and dying constantly to educate and create a forum where they can express and share their fears, sadness, anger, etc. It is critical that support continues for the grieving children without necessarily pushing them too fast out of it. Depending on the relationship the child had with the deceased, grief may linger on beyond the funeral and other rituals that may follow. It is at that point that some children will start asking all kinds of unanswered questions popping up from different situations around them. It is very important to remember too that from this time forth, children who have experienced grief in the loss of a loved one might suddenly become fearful of more losses whenever another loved one falls sick or is injured. The surviving parent, siblings or other relatives and friends need to be patient, loving and compassionate in comforting them with assurance that all will be well. The child has reasons to doubt such words and so it is everyone's responsibility to assure them in a realistic way that the sick person could either get better or die. The most important thing is to be forthright and truthful in a language and method that is clear and appropriate to their level of understanding. Overprotecting the children and hiding the truth is not helpful and not only complicates their grieving process, but also their growth and development process. Let the surviving parent of the grieving child maintain daily routines like bed-time, meal-time and scheduled activities and games. Make an effort to hug, hold or cuddle the child as often as possible. Be patient and tolerant with them when they exhibit some regressive behaviors like thumb sucking or wetting their beds even though they had already stopped that. Encourage them to express their feelings and emotions in a healthy way as you share your own in an open and honest way with them. As you do this, you are telling them that their feelings are normal and genuine, so they do not need to be ashamed of them. When you do not have an answer for their questions, tell them in a simple and clear language that you simply don't have an answer, but sit with them and be really present to their emotional needs. Do not dodge their questions or confusion If the child unexpectedly explodes and acts in some unacceptable way, don't react in anger or punish them. Instead, address the behavior and slowly but carefully explore the feelings and thoughts.

10

Teenagers adn Grief – Helping Them To Cope

At every stage in life, grief can be unbearable, especially in the loss to death of a parent or a close guardian. It is even harder during the adolescent years when one is crossing from childhood to the turbulent years of young adulthood. The teenagers may experience the overwhelming loss of someone who helped shape their still fragile self identities. They may go through serious episodes of total confusion, anger, feelings of rejection and abandonment by a parent at a time when they need them most. These feelings about death will be part of their permanent history for ever. For lack of understanding, they may go into stages of questioning why their parent "gave in" and perhaps died of a disease that a friend's parent may have endured or survived like cancer etc. We have to remember that their own understanding is limited. Where a death has resulted from bad habits or lifestyle like alcohol, drugs and substance abuse, the anger and blame may be even worse. They translate it that their parent or elder sibling who was their anchor or support was not loving or caring enough to live for them. This anger also destroys trust for others in their lives. It may cause them to distance themselves in self protection and preservation from similar future heartache.

As the teens struggle with all these emotions or grief and bereavement, many things are likely to go wrong. The academic performance may suddenly drop as well as their morale or motivation. They lack focus, concentration and a sense of direction. The teen may struggle in his anger, feeling that if his life will ever improve or makes a meaning, it will have to be squarely dependent on him. For this reason, he or she might make drastic changes and completely drown themselves on a journey to achieve and live their dreams since there is now nobody else to do so. This is more so when the deceased parent was their favorite one. They may even go to the extent of emotionally and psychologically blocking out everyone else and simply withdrawing from everything and everyone for lack of trust on others.

Unfortunately, even through the season of grieving, the adolescent will still be undergoing the normal psychological, physiological, academic and all other pressures relevant to his age. They may already be undergoing pressure from all sides to "grow up" and facing the challenge of leaving the security of childhood and home, to face the wide unknown world of challenges galore without the protection of the departed parent. The scary process of separation from parents, siblings and family may already have begun and rocked the boat of life. They are already anxious and fearful. Then suddenly their guide, their mentor and their point of reference suddenly dies. Whether the deceased parent has been sick for sometime or not, to a teenager, especially experiencing the death of a loved one for the very first time, this must appear sudden and unexpected.

With the death of a parent, the pressure is heightened as everyone starts calling upon the teenager to pull themselves up and learn to be a "good/strong" support for the surviving parent. They are quickly reminded that they are no longer children, yet on the other hand they are not fully acknowledged as adults. The may go through moments of overwhelming feelings and pressure from every side. Unless handled with loving care and compassionate understanding, this can be a dangerous time where suicide may become a contemplated option. They begin to hear comments like "You need to be a strong role model for your younger siblings and show them how to survive. You must grow up fast and carry on your father/mother's legacy". Contrary to this, the teenager is longing and wishing for the return of their newly deceased parent or elder sibling. They are not interested with carrying on with anybody's legacy. Often time, for lack of knowledge, many adults discourage teens from mourning or sharing their grief openly.

What the teenagers yearn for during their grief or bereavement is that adults be open, honest and loving so they can effectively help them learn both the joy and pain that comes from caring deeply for others. Feeling dazed and numb at the death of a loved one is a normal part of the teens' grieving process just as it is for everyone else. The numbness helps emotions to catch up and face the reality of their loss at a safe gradual pace that is comfortable and specific to each individual as always. The numbness also insulates them from hearing or experiencing too much too quickly of what they don't want to hear. It is wrong to assume that the grieving adolescent has more than enough friends or family support for this transition and therefore leave them out when caring for their grieving parents or younger siblings. This only fuels the anger and feelings of rejection and needs to be addressed and attended to before it is too late. These are social expectations and assumptions that we all need to be sensitive to or careful with.

The teenagers are often pushed into roles of care for the surviving parents and younger siblings (even surviving grandparents) without permission, encouragement or space to mourn or grieve their own losses. Unless their teenage friends have undergone personal losses and grief, they will be of little or no support. Instead they might even ignore the subject of loss completely from their conversations because it makes them uneasy and they don't know how to handle it. Nobody needs to hear words or comments like "Since we cannot change this situation, you just need to grow up and move on with life as best as you can". Worse still is when a parent dies and the surviving family has to move into a smaller unfamiliar home or apartment on their own or with other family members. These may even be people they never related with closely or well and only God knows how they will survive. I have known international families from different cultures and other parts of the world who have lost a loved one, be it a parent, a spouse or one's child. The trauma that goes with this kind of a situation cannot be described in any adequate words. Their grief is multiplied many times over, as they organize finances, air tickets, disposing of their household goods, at times even those of sentimental value and personal memorabilia as they cannot afford to ship them back to their home country on top of the expensive air tickets for themselves and the remains of their loved one. I cannot even try to imagine the agony of two teenage children and their father, having lived in a foreign land for most of these children's lives now going back without their mother to help them settle back in their families and communities where they have not been for over 10 years. It must be even harder for the widower who must also find his way back home alone in tears and grief while he went abroad in search of education and a better life for his family, hoping to return home loaded with all the good things they all dreamt of together. This is what would truly be unfathomable grief and disorientation for each of them.

However, as time passes, those caring for the teens must watch out for the following symptoms and act before it is too late.

- Chronic depression, sleeplessness, restlessness and poor self esteem.

- Poor academic performance or lack of interest for school activities, even the ones they enjoyed before.

- Risk taking behaviors such as alcohol and drug abuse, fighting, rudeness, sexual experimentation, loss of appetite or sudden overeating.

- Denying pain and acting overly mature and "OK"

It may be necessary to look for school counselors, church groups or even a private grief therapist. Provide the grieving teenager with safe and nurturing outlets for this season of his life which he too cannot quite understand. Give them permission to grieve and vent as necessary. Be willing to stand by them as best and as closely as possible during their healing or reconstruction process. Teenagers cannot choose between grieving and not grieving. As you willingly, compassionately and lovingly walk with the adolescent through their grieving journey, you are giving the best gift ever. *The Gift of Yourself,* which may be the ultimate gift of healing for them. You will help alleviate feelings of abandonment, insecurity, low self esteem, shock and anger and give them a sense of relief and your much needed companionship.

While there are all kinds of support systems for the grieving students, there is a very special role for the teachers, school mates and classmates. School is in reality, a home away from home, especially because students spend three quarters of their waking time in the school communities. It can therefore be a place of refuge, offering a stabilizing environment where they can openly share their feelings of fear and anger without necessarily being ridiculed or asked to suddenly grow up and take care of others. It would help if you can earn their trust and be able to come down to whatever level they are in life, look them in the eye and tell them "I am here for you and willing to help you through your grief as best as I can . I know you and I can count on a few other teachers and students who feel for you and want to support you".

Your effectiveness as a school teacher or counselor will largely depend on how much you know and how current you are on the subject of death and dying. This is a topic that most of us would rather not get involved in unless it becomes a real necessity. It may also cause you to delve into your own life's journey to know when and how you dealt with death in your own family, and its impact on you, especially if you were still a child. This will better equip you to be a better help for grieving students. But this calls you to be intentional in how you relate with your students, taking every opportunity to reflect on matters of life and death. Occasions like the birth of a new baby in the family, the death of a grandparent, the death of a pet, or a friend will help open up conversations on this topic. Dr. Alan D. Wolfelt, Ph.D. calls these *"Teachable Moments"* and *"Created Moments"* of addressing issues of life and death as well as grief and bereavement. This also helps break up the barriers to discussing death. We need to help our children grow knowing the reality that when death strikes it is both natural and permanent. This knowledge will be an important pillar of support when they need it most and with no time to prepare.

Harder still is the unexpected death of a classmate that suddenly tells them that they too carry the potential to die young. In the healing/recovery process, you might encourage the students to make drawings or write letters give to the deceased student's parents. This will not only help the students in their grief process, but also the grieving family. At some point some students may need further counseling if their grief becomes complicated and prolonged. Consider wisely referring them to a professional counselor with vast experience in counseling traumatized children and students.

- Be a good observer in order to detect behavioral and personality changes that might need quick intervention.

- Be patient. The teens may appear confused or even disoriented.

- Be honest and don't lie to them about death Let them know its finality and permanence

- Allow them to grieve at their own pace, individually or in groups if it will help them deal with their loss of a common friend.

11

Un-Acknowledged Grief or Non-Bereavement Losses.

Just as much as God is no respecter of persons, death has a definite date with everyone born of woman and man. The bible tells us that God sends rain to everyone on the earth, both rich and poor. Grief is another thing in life that strikes whoever loses a loved one to death. Regardless of the kind of life they led, everyone's death is likely to bring grief and pain to somebody somewhere. It may be a parent or family whose son or daughter has killed another person, intentionally or accidentally and ended up executed or committed to serve a life sentence for their crime. The family of the victim and the family of the criminal will both face issues of grief. Needless to say, the victim's family will be dealing with deep anger and loss. As much as is possible, they will receive grief and other support from family and friends, known and even unknown sympathizers. And when such a case is exposed to the public through media covering, they will receive emotional, spiritual, moral and even material support from near and far away On the contrary, the family of the accused criminal, however good they may be in their community, will more often than not experience condemnation, isolation, resentment and rejection from everyone around them. Because of the anger that goes with this, they will probably receive very little sympathy or consolation for their own loss. They will also not feel comfortable grieving their loss openly. I can only imagine any parent or child going through this kind of grief.

Another un-acknowledged grief would result from the family of one who kills their parent(s) or sibling(s) and is subsequently sentenced to death. The immediate family will have a double tragedy because not only have they lost the initial murdered victim, but they will end up losing the second family member who did the killing. In the case of one who kills their parent(s), any surviving siblings will go through the untold agony of dealing with the loss of their parents and eventually a sibling either to execution or to prison for life. Yes they will be angry at the loss of their parent(s) and perhaps receive emotional and other support for their loss, but people will find it hard to console them for losing their sibling too. Their anger too, may inhibit them from dealing with their grief in a healthy way. Worse still is the grief of any living grandparents of such a child who painfully not only lose their own child but subsequently their grandchild. This kind of grief has the potential to bring them to an early death. These are some of the unresolved family dynamics that end up exploding in the most unexpected consequences, places and times.

Just as much as life is diverse in every respect, so are there as many reasons for grief as you can ever imagine. Think of a parent whose child young or adult has committed murder or other serious crimes that commits him to prison for life without parole, after several years of waiting or even trying to fight for his life. It has often been the case that in such instances, especially where the serious crime is obvious that almost everyone gives up on the person in question. But the parents will hang in there with their son or daughter until the final verdict is given. They will then enter into their own emotional prison of grieving and mourning their child behind their own home prison doors. The sad reality is that while those whose child is dead and buried will have some form of closure, mourn and receive grief support, these parents receive little or no support or sympathy for their loss. This loss also carries more anger and guilt at times for what their child will have done. I have had an encounter with such parents who were looking for a support group that would be willing to walk with them. Apparently, there are support groups for those whose children are in prisons but very rarely for such parents as described above. The closest support one might find for them is if their pastors or church are kind and understanding enough to help them at least through the initial phase of a grief which they must endure for the rest of their lives.

A young teenage girl may become pregnant and decide to abort the baby to conceal the event in fear of the immediate consequences from parents or looking at the long term responsibility for which she is not prepared. She is mostly unaware of the after effects and naively assumes that life will go back to normal immediately. Unfortunately, a few days later she is not only consumed with guilt, but also by a deep sense of unexplainable grief and sadness. She may try all she can to look and play well as always, but this can become an unacknowledged secret grief that could lead into depression and numerous other disorders. It may haunt her any time she sees a child known to have been born around the same time she aborted her own.

The same scenario may involve a woman who for many reasons, from financial, complicated family dynamics etc. which she feels are not conducive to having a baby or more children, decides to go through an abortion. Without justifying abortion, the reality is that at some point in her life sooner or later, she will have to face the reality of her emotions, loss, grief and painful absence of a baby that she never saw or held in her hands. This too may become an unending grief, especially if later in life any of the above categories of women decide to have a baby, but cannot due to complications from the abortion. If nobody knows about this, she will for ever be judged and even laughed at for her "self-induced" barrenness.

Miscarriages and still births are other deaths that result in deep grief but often very little emotional support is given to the grieving parents. Many people assume that since the pregnancy was only a few weeks or months old it's no big deal. And so it is, that while a mother & father who lost an infant or toddler is surrounded by much love, support and sympathy from family and friends, this other family fades into the cracks to grieve their loss alone or with only a brief support.

Yet again, they too will often remember their loss at the sight of a child born around the same time theirs own baby would have been born. But because of the reactions of those around them, often resulting from the common discomfort of dealing with any form of death, they too will behave like all is well in public but weep alone at night or in secret places without sharing their pain and grief with anyone. They will have no little grave spots to visit and come to terms with their loss, and very rarely any pictures or memorials for the baby. Thank God for advanced grief support systems that are now helping make some memorial pictures, foot/hand prints of the little babies born too early to survive and even allowing such parents to spend some bonding time with their little babies beautifully dressed. Some of these parents have called for chaplains to do a memorial service for their little ones, praying for them and their families that God will sustain them in their journeys ahead. This also goes for full term babies who for one reason or other pass away.

The hardest part of my ministry in the Labor and Delivery units is watching a family that arrived in the delivery room with little baby clothes, cameras on the ready and baby's car seat, only to watch them carry everything back home but

without the long awaited baby. I watched helplessly at a couple who arrived at the ER as the wife was having serious abdominal aches. They were quickly told that they were in the process of losing a baby they never knew they were expecting in the first place. The baby was born and when the man was offered a chance to see his little baby son (the mother did not want to see the baby), he was heard telling the little baby to look out for his older brother who had died at the age of 7 a year earlier from a previous marriage. The explosion of his unresolved previous grief was because his ex-wife had full custody of their deceased son and so he had not attended the funeral. His un-acknowledged grief came as a shock to his grieving wife who knew nothing about it until then. Until that moment, his grieving wife said that while they both tried to rest and come to terms with their loss, she had heard him silently asking God "why me, why have you done this to me ***again.*** She said that all along she felt confused but was now able to understand and console her husband who was now handling double grief.

Rape, incest and increasingly sodomy victim must deal with one of the most painful grief and loss, where one cannot openly share or express their emotions and heartache.

The secret grief of having someone forcefully take complete charge/control of one's body must be one of the most painful experiences. This often results in self blame, condemnation and judgment and worse still potentially dangerous impact on any future relationships. Alongside the deep grief is also being blamed for the rape by those who get to know about it of what you did or did not do to bring it upon oneself. If the rape/sodomy victim gets married later and hides the incident from their spouse, this could have very adverse effects on their marriage. In some unfortunate cases, the victims have taken out of their anger by becoming abusers themselves. Grieving such pain in secrecy has deprived millions of victims healing support and sympathy because of their fear of being hurt further by people's reactions. The worst is in cases of incest where a father abuses a daughter, and when the daughter reports this to the mother or guardian, the whole matter is hushed up as if it never happened. The victim is not only threatened by the abuser never to tell anyone or face dire consequences including death, but receives similar treatment from her mother. For some such victims, their deep secret grief has become their close companion till death.

Worse still is the grief experienced by a couple expecting their first child only to lose it to a miscarriage or a still birth because of one complication or another. The saddest part is that from the first time they become aware of their expected baby, their mindset completely changes to adapt to their new roles. They start thinking of names, anticipating the gender of the baby and many other fantasies as to how their baby would look like, and all the things they would do together as a family as he grew up. Some start arranging the baby's room, buying baby clothes and books. Then suddenly there is a miscarriage or the baby with only a few more weeks to go is born dead or dies in the birthing process. The agony that these parents undergo is unexplainable and their grief inconsolable. The same painful experiences go for grandparents who had excitedly awaited their grand child with great anticipation. My ministry to such families as the chaplain for a hospital's labor and delivery unit is the hardest. As a mother myself, I can never find appropriate words to address their sorrow as the tiny little babies are brought to the mother to hold and cuddle before they leave the hospital. The thought of a mother who came to deliver her baby, bringing the dainty blue or pink baby clothes plus a new baby's car seat, but now going back home alone in tears is the most heartbreaking scenario. The unfortunate thing is that many people have no clue how deep the pain of such parents must be. Most people assume that since the miscarried or still born baby had not lived among them, she or he will not be missed as much as a two or ten years old baby.

The reality is quite on the contrary as they leave a deep vacuum that even their future babies cannot fill.

These parents might not even have a grave spot to visit in the future for their baby. They may have photos taken before the infant's body is left at the hospital for burial. In some cases of miscarriage only a few weeks into the pregnancy, there will be no chance to hold the baby at all and they will always miss that bonding moment. It may take them a great many months and years to come to terms with that loss.

Job losses and loss of one's identity and livelihood have increasingly become a major and traumatic challenge to many individuals. Nobody is exempted, regardless of age, career path of social status. Gone are the days when one would almost automatically, if so desired, expect or hope to work towards planned retirement in careers like teaching, management and administration, etc. In the past, with adequate education, training, self-discipline and good work ethics, one could more easily chart one's career path, possible or anticipated promotions, etc. one could even at times be able to forecast what retirement will be like financially etc. Unfortunately, the work life and environment have drastically changed and very few people can comfortably achieve their retirement goals and expectations. It is not a surprise that a lot more elderly people continue working to earn their basic living long after their retirement age. Many such people silently grieve the loss of their retirement dreams of going on vacations, on cruises, doing things for and with their grandchildren, or simply affording a comfortable life without having to depend on their children or welfare handouts. As much as the companies and corporations are downsizing the workforce, so are families and individuals being forced to cut down their expenses in order to survive. The sad reality and grief is that people are now *surviving* instead of living.

In a nutshell, there is little or no job security assured to any employee. When you hear of an employee being laid off from work from as early as 40 years of age, with a young family, a mortgage and perhaps multiple healthcare issues in the family, you can only imagine the devastation and grief that this must bring to the entire family. The parents of this employee might have been dependent on them as their own health starts to fail and on the other hand might now be compelled by circumstances to start sharing their retirement savings to help raise their grandchildren. It is therefore only fair to say that the loss of a job can be a serious vicious cycle or traumatic experiences, not just to the employee and breadwinner, but to all other people dependent on him for one need or another. Feelings of anger and inadequacy lead to depression, withdrawal and grief over their losses. They may end up feeling compelled to make a lot of forced adjustments to their lifestyles.

12

COPING WITH GRIEF:

Picking up the Pieces of our Broken Lives

It is hard to think of where one begins on this topic considering the drastic and permanent changes that the death of a loved one brings in our lives, regardless of how young or old. It is even harder to know when the healing and coping with one's grief ever begins, bearing in mind that every day brings new waves of sadness, emptiness, anger, questions and a roller coaster of emotions. Part of the anger against others may be that perhaps they could have done something to save the life of the deceased. Again, Jesus gives us permission to weep when touched by the jugged splintered edges of grief, pain and sorrow as found in Martha and Mary at the death of Christ's friend and their brother, Lazarus. Christ has a tender heart that hurts with us. At our lowest and saddest moments, Christ sits with us, holds us and weeps with us. He grieves with us and compassionately comforts us in times of unbearable grief, sorrow and despair. Once again, we must remember that this phase too will be very personal and there are no set standards or length of time by which this must begin. With time and with God's understanding and help, you will survive this. He will help you forge a new relationship with the one who has gone ahead of you. Grief is part of the healing process.

The following are suggestions and guidelines from which different people can find help based on where they are with their kind of grief. I would encourage each of us to do what is best for them and their situations and therefore adjust these ideas to suit them. One's faith in God plays a major role of support and encouragement. It may be quiet prayer or meditation, religious services and ceremonies, or other activities at your place of worship. Do not push yourself too hard but be moderate with expectations upon self. There may be moments, however, when you might feel angry with God, even wonder where God was when this tragedy happened, even wondering whether He caused it, etc. The most encouraging thing at such a time is to remember that God is big enough to love and accept you as well as your anger. Be honest with God – He can handle it. One of the most consoling things to remember is that Jesus knows and understands the real pain of grief and loss. In Mark 15 verse 34 Jesus cried out to His Father just before he gave up His soul. *"My God, my God, why have you forsaken me"*? At that point on the cross when Christ took upon Him all our sins and transgressions, His father could not bear it and looked away from His son for a moment. He experienced the deep sorrow then and so fully understands our pain even when it is too deep or painful for us to express it.

In John 11:35 "Jesus Wept" when He was told that His good friend Lazarus had died. This way He gave us permission to weep when touched by the jugged, splintered edges of grief, pain and sorrow. It reminds us that Christ too has a tender heart and fully understands our heartache at a moment of grief. At our lowest and saddest moment, Christ sits with us, holds us and weeps with us. He grieves with us and comforts us in times of unbearable grief and despair. In John 11 verses 25-26,

"So shall thy barns be filled with plenty, and your vats will overflow with new wine." This is one of the blessings promised to obedience, (Deut. 28:1-2, 8), so that no one becomes poorer for honoring the Lord with his possessions, as the unbeliever thinks. God shall be no man's debtor: He shall more than repay that which is given to Him, when it is given with the proper attitude. It is to be carefully noted that this promise is not given just to him who "gives" to the Lord, but only to him who "honors" the Lord with His possessions. There can be a great difference.

God You Said....
- Better is a little with righteousness, than vast revenues without justice. *(Proverbs 16:8)*

If the Christian Entrepreneur has the Lord's righteousness, it matters little what else they may not have, for as soon as this short life is over they go on to eternal riches with the Lord. But to possess great wealth without righteousness is to only generate a taste for luxury which shall be eternally unsatisfied after death. The greatest possessions that one may own fades into nothingness in the light of a Christless eternity, yet many are daily selling their souls for the revenues of the earth.

God You Said....
- Better is a little with the fear of the Lord, than great treasure with trouble. *(Proverbs 15:16)*

The "fear of the Lord," which involves salvation, is the supreme treasure, for if the Christian Entrepreneur only has a "little" of this world's goods with it, they are still supremely rich in that they are an heir of the world that is to come, and so rich beyond imagination in things which cannot be taken away. Riches, so far from averting, brings trouble in acquiring, defending, administering, and losing them. It is therefore far better to have little of the world, and to keep communion with God, and enjoy Him in it, and live by faith, than to have the greatest plenty and live without God in the world. Many of the worlds richest Entrepreneurs, while possessing great riches, are not rich towards God. The Christian Entrepreneur must trust God for the riches the He has assigned to them.

God You Said….
- By humility and the fear of the Lord are riches and honor and life. *(Proverbs 22:4)*

Riches, honor and life are the chief desires of almost all Christian Entrepreneurs, but the problem lies in how they attain them. Too many have no scruples about how these are obtained, and so they violate the Scriptural means of attaining them, which is by humility and reverential fear of the Lord. Our Lord repeated this same order for obtaining these things in Matthew 6:33. Humility and the fear of the Lord always go together, for humility is necessary before one can truly reverence the Lord. Proverbs 15:33 and 18:12 have already established this order. Many Entrepreneurs desire riches so that they will not have to be humble.

God You Said….
- He who has a slack hand becomes poor, but the hand of the diligent makes rich. *(Proverbs 10:4)*

The Christian Entrepreneur cannot think that God's promised provision is meant to encourage slothfulness and idleness, for diligence in their labor is God's means of giving them their needs. Someone has wisely observed that God generally gives most to the most diligent and most faithful workers. Parallel teaching is found in Proverbs 13:4 and 19:15. Hard labor has been man's decreed lot since he sinned in Eden, (Genesis 3:17-19), but it can be blessed to the enrichment of man by the Lord, where a man's ways pleases the Lord. All attempts to get rich without honest labor are simply man's denial of his sinfulness, and his attempt to bypass the curse. Labor is meant to remind man of his sinfulness.

God You Said….
- Riches do not profit in the day of wrath, but righteousness delivers from death. *(Proverbs 11:4)*

The Christian Entrepreneur is warned that at best, riches serve men only in this world, but the closer men come to death, the less value riches have. Righteousness on the other hand which means, a right relationship to God—has eternal profit. This is what the Christian Entrepreneur wants to be consume with – eternal profit.

God You Said....

- For riches are not forever, nor does a crown endure to all generations. *(Proverbs 27:24)*

The Christian Entrepreneur will either manage money or money will manage them. Solomon, known for his wisdom and wealth, recorded five timeless principles of money management in Proverbs:

- Accounting (v.23) – "know the state of your flocks" refers to diligence in record keeping. In modern times, this means keeping track of what we own, owe, earn, and spend.

- Planning (21:5) – Planning how we will spend money is essential to good stewardship. Planned spending brings satisfaction, but "impulse spending" can have devastating consequences.

- Saving (21:20) – the idea of "treasure" in the house of the wise implies that resources have been saved and will be available when we need them.

- Contentment (15:16) – we are deceived if we think having more riches or pleasure will make us happy. Scripture encourages us to enjoy what we have now without desiring to get more.

- Giving (3:9,10) – honoring God with the first of our income and resources establishes His reign in our lives and begins a divine cycle of blessing.

God You Said....

- He who trusts in his riches will fall, but the righteous will flourish like foliage. (*Proverbs 11:28*)

This is so because riches are so undependable, but who so trust in the Lord shall not only be righteous, but shall flourish in His righteous. The evergreen tree has long been fitly used as a symbol of the saint, (Psalm 1:3; Jeremiah 17:7-8). A branch does not live of its own intrinsic life, but must be attached to the root (Col. 2:6-10).

Things To Remember

1. The main reason for transfer of wealth is so that the Christian Entrepreneur can finance the Kingdom.

2. The goal is to get your money to work for you as you continue to work for God.

3. Remember that wisdom is more important than money.

4. Remember that righteousness is more important than money.

5. Remember that fearing God is more important than money.

6. God uses money to strengthen our trust in Him.

7. God uses money to develop our trustworthiness.

8. God uses money to prove His love (Matthew 7:11).

9. God uses money to demonstrate His faithfulness.

10. God use money to unite Christians in blessings.

11. God uses money to cultivate self-control.

12. God uses money to clarify spiritual maturity.

13. Listen to Your Self-Talk.

Chapter 11

THE CHRISTIAN ENTREPRENEUR & EXPECTATION

How do we show our expectation? In what ways do we make it evident that we are expecting what the Word declares we can have. Notice Hebrews 10:23. "Let us hold fast the confession of our expectation without wavering; for he is faithful that promised." The King James translation employs the word "faith" but it is not the Greek word pistis which is usually translated "faith".

The word here is the one I have been sharing, the word "expectation". You are encouraged to hold fast the confession of your expectation "without wavering". Now there are two things you can immediately learn from this, and the first is that it is possible to waver. Don't fool yourself, it is very possible to waver: your best friend will try to get you off the Word, Satan will try to get you off the Word, the society in which you live will try to get you off the truths of the Word.

God knows that it is very easy to waver, and this is why He reminds the Christian Entrepreneur of their part, "Let us hold fast..." There is no automatic protection from wavering which becomes yours at salvation; it takes work. You and I have the privilege of deciding if we are going to hold fast. And if we want results, then we must hold fast without wavering. This is a powerful truth, yet it is possible because God has never asked you to do one thing that is not possible for you to do.

Let us, the believers, the Christian Entrepreneurs, "hold fast the confession of our expectation without wavering." The word "confession" is a translation of the Greek word homologia -- homo means "like" and logia comes from logos, "a word or saying". It means "to say a like word", or as I like to express it, "to say the same as the Word says", agreeing with the Word. The English word that gives a more preferable translation is the word "confession", not the traditional form of religious confession, but a confession with the mouth that agrees with the Word. Notice a similar form of the same word in Romans 10:10: "With the mouth confession is made unto salvation. "

Your expectation will show itself by your speech and by your actions; your talk and your walk. Everything you do will either show that you are expecting what God has said you can have in the Word or that you do not really expect it will come to pass. God exhorts you to "hold fast", not just keep up appearances but "hold fast to the confession of your expectation without wavering." And why should you hold fast to it? "For he is faithful that promised." It is God that promised it, and when God promises something, it is guaranteed. Now you must say what the Word says, not what the circumstances seem to say, not what the economy says, not even what your wife or husband, your best friends, or your neighbors say. This is one vital way in which you demonstrate the fact that you are expecting results. Now if you do not believe the Word, if you do not believe the law of believing, you will not talk about it. But if you really believe it, then your expectation will come into manifestation by saying what the Word says.

Whatever I am expecting will come out in my confession. If I am expecting the worst to happen, sooner or later I am going to confess it. If I am expecting to be bankrupt by the end of the year, sooner or later in my conversation it is going to come out that I am short of cash, that I have a liquidity problem. But if I am expecting the very best, sooner or later it is going to come out in my conversation that the very best is just around the corner. "Let us hold fast the confession of our expectation without wavering." Why should you waver? Because suddenly you are flooded with bills or there is a credit squeeze and nobody is going to buy anything this month? You are solidly standing on God's Word and are operating the principles it teaches. There is no need for wavering; it will only occur when you take your eyes off the Word and get them on people or circumstances around you. So long as you are totally convinced that you are poised and balanced in Christ, poised to the point of being on tiptoe in expectation and yet firmly balanced on the Word, there is no need to waver. It is when you are not convinced that you start wavering.

Most believers get tricked by Satan because they waver on this matter of expectation, because they are not 100 per cent convinced. Now if you want results, expectation will work every time. All you need to do is operate the law of believing and "hold fast the confession of your expectation without wavering". And why should we do this? The word "for" always tells us why a statement is true, "for he is faithful that promised." Does the Word mean what it says and says what it means? Is the Word reliable? Can I place my life, my future, my finances on the Word? Does the Word really work? If you are convinced it does, then you can, as it were, run a successful business that brings glory to God. Now this is what the Word teaches: you show forth your expectation by confession, saying what the Word says.

Another example of the usage of the word "confession" is in 1 Timothy 6:12: "Fight the good fight of faith, lay hold on eternal life, whereunto thou art also called, and hast confessed a good confession before many witnesses." This is what we must do, for words can work wonders on the one hand and words can work blunders on the other hand. A good confession of our expectation is based on God's Word. If God says it, that's sufficient.

"If you confess with your mouth Jesus as Lord, and shall believe in your heart that God raised him from the dead, thou shalt be saved. For with the heart man believes unto righteousness, and with the mouth confession is made, unto salvation" (Romans 10:9-10). In both verses 9 and 10, the exhortation is to confess with the mouth. The word "confess" is homologeo, to agree with the Word in your speech. But first you must believe in your heart, the seat of the personal life. Believing is an assumption, and you assume that when the Word states that God raised Jesus from the dead, it is correct. You were not there, but you assume it to be so, you confess it, and you are saved. Because Christ died for your sins, then you are free from sin, and you are a son of God. This is how you were saved.

Now notice Colossians 2:6: "As you have therefore received Christ Jesus the Lord, so walk ye in him." Here we have a comparison introduced by the little words "as" and "so". In the same way in which you received Christ Jesus the Lord, you must walk in Him. We have just read in Romans 10:9 that you receive Christ by believing and confession, agreeing with the Word. Now in Colossians it teaches us to continue living the Christian life, the walk, in the same way -- by believing and confession. "As ye have therefore received Christ Jesus the Lord, so walk ye in him." How do you receive anything from God? You believe and you confess.

The totality of the Christian Entrepreneurs life is based on believing, which is action, and the renewing of the mind so that the confession from your lips agrees with the Word. Now since confession is saying what the Word says, when God says in Philippians 4:19, "My God shall supply all your need", are you going to say what the Word says, "My God is supplying all my need." If you will do your part in expectation, God is going to do His part, so that at the time of receiving there will be an abundance, which is God's will for every Christian Entrepreneur.

God You Said…..
- Call to Me, and I will answer you, and show you great and mighty things, which you do not know. *(Jeremiah 33:3)*

The positive assurance from God is that if we will call on Him, He will answer us in ways that will astound us. Call to the Lord, and ask Him to show you things beyond your own ability to perceive. The Christian Entrepreneur has to know that the positive assurance from God is that if they call on Him, He will answer them in ways that will astound them and their businesses.

The Christian Entrepreneur must call to the Lord, and ask Him to show him or her things beyond their own ability to perceive, such as where are the customers, where are the opportunities, where is the money, where are the resources, what demographic area should I concentrate on, etc.?

God You Said....

- Ask, and it will be given to you; seek, and you will find; knock, and it will be opened to you. For everyone who asks receives, and he who seeks finds, and to him who knocks it will be opened. *(Matthew 7:7-8)*

The Greek imperatives, ask, seek, and knock are in the present tense, suggesting continued petition. The Entrepreneurs faith needs to be Active - Ask, Seek, Knock!, not passive. Asking - implies humility and a consciousness of need. Seeking - Is Asking & Acting. Knocking - Is asking, plus acting, plus persevering! The phrases signify to seek with earnestness, and diligence, and perseverance. The promise is, that what we seek shall be given us. It is of course implied that we seek with a proper spirit, with humility, sincerity, and perseverance. It is implied, also, that we ask for the things which may be consistent for God to give--that is, things which He has promised to give, and which would be best for us and His kingdom.

God You Said....

- A man's gift makes room for him, and brings him before great men. *(Proverbs 18:16)*

This gift is not a bribe, but and asset or talent which opens the way. The Christian Entrepreneur needs to find his or her gift and focus on it. Focus on what you're good at. Your gift will enlarge your acquaintances, gain you respect among men and bring you before great men.

God You Said....

- And you shall remember the Lord your God, for it is He who gives you power to get wealth, that He may establish His covenant which He swore to your fathers, as it is this day. *(Deuteronomy 8:18)*

The word power means; vigor, strength, force, capacity, wealth, means or substance.

a. **Remember the Lord your God**: In times of abundance, it is so easy to forget the Lord - or at least no longer seek Him with the urgency we once had! The Christian Entrepreneur is to remember that God is the author of their beings and the God of their lives.

b. **It is He who gives you power to get wealth**: yes, you have worked hard. Yes, you are brilliant. Yes, you are talented. But who gave you the body, the brain, and the talent? It is all of God! For though men may have seeming opportunities for getting wealth, may have capacities for the management of business for the acquisition of it, and may not be wanting in diligence and industry, yet may not attain it; it is the blessing of God that makes rich, and to that it should be imputed whenever it is enjoyed.

c. **That He may establish His covenant**: remember *why* God has blessed you - that it would ultimately further *His* eternal purpose. So are you using your material blessing to further that purpose - or, are you hoarding it unto yourself?

God You Said....

- For when God made a promise to Abraham, because He could swear by no one greater, He swore by Himself, saying, surely blessing I will bless you, and multiplying I will multiply you. And so, after he had patiently endured, he obtained the promise. *(Hebrews 6:13-15)*

We have in God and in His expressed purpose to bless us in Christ, grounds for confident expectation. The fulfillment of His promise to Abraham provides assurance that He is certain to perform what He promises.

God You Said....

- But you, when you pray, go into your room, and when you have shut your door, pray to your Father who is in the secret place; and your Father who sees in secret will reward you openly. *(Matthew 6:6)*

God rewards genuine prayer. He knows the motives of our hearts and rewards us accordingly. He will miss no point of reward. This reward may be the reward of answered prayer.

For the Christian Entrepreneur there has to be some place to which he or she may resort where no ear will hear them but His ear, and no eye can see them but His eye. Unless there is such a place, a secret prayer life will not be long or strictly maintained.

God You Said....

- The Lord will command the blessing on you in your storehouses and in all to which you set your hand, and He will bless you in the land which the Lord your God is giving you. *(Deuteronomy 28:8)*

God will bless the Christian Entrepreneur, if they do their duty and are not idle.

The Lord Jehovah, the Eternal God, has a good plan for you. His greatest desire is to bless you. He, therefore, has opened His mouth to speak well of you, pronouncing His divine benediction over you. In the traditional worship service, the benediction is the final blessing that the minister of God speaks over his people. Likewise, the Lord's blessing is the final word for the Christian Entrepreneur. In fact, He has commanded His liberal and abundant prosperity to come to you. He wants you to have so much that it heaps together in your storehouses.

The Lord has also blessed your hands with power and strength. He has given you the direction for your life and the means to follow His instructions. Your hands hold dominion and bounty. Whatever you set them to will prosper and your business will be greatly benefited. Whenever you send forth and sow your seed, you will see abundant harvest returning to you at the proper and opportune time. The land and the fields that God has given you will bring forth liberal crops, amply supplying your every need, for the Lord God has charged it to do so, without fail.

God You Said....

- And we know that all things work together for good to those who love God, to those who are the called according to His purpose. *(Romans 8:28)*

a. And we know that all things work together for good: God's sovereignty and ability to manage every aspect of our lives is demonstrated in the fact that all things work together for good to those who love God, though we must face *the sufferings of this present time* (Romans 8:18). God is able to even make those sufferings work together for our good and His good.

b. God is able to work *all* things together, not some things. He works them for good together, not in isolation. This promise is for those who love God in the biblical understanding of love. The Christian Entrepreneur knows that God will manage the affairs of their life because they are called according to His purpose.

God You Said....
• You will be blessed when you come in and blessed when you go out. *(Deuteronomy 28:6)*

All your enterprises will have good success. Based on the word of God, the Christian Entrepreneur is preserved from the dangers of the world and should have comforts of their condition. This blessing should attend them in their business journeys, going out and coming in. Their business will be protected, and the business affairs they go after should succeed well. The Christian Entrepreneur must continue to realize that they need God at every turn, he or she will not be safe if God withdraws His protection, or suspends His favor.

God You Said....
• For I know the thoughts that I think toward you, says the Lord, thoughts of peace and not of evil, to give you a future and a hope. Then you will call upon Me and go and pray to Me, and I will listen to you. And you will seek Me and find Me, when you search for Me with all your heart. *(Jeremiah 29:11-13)*

We're all encouraged by a leader who stirs us to move ahead; someone who believes we can do the task he has given and who will be with us all the way. God is that kind of leader. He knows the future, and His plans for us are good and full of hope. As long as God, who knows the future, provides our agenda and goes with us as we fulfill His mission, we the Christian Entrepreneur can have boundless hope. This does not mean that we will be spared pain, suffering, or hardship, but that God will see us through to a glorious conclusion. God did not forget His people, even though they were captive in Babylon. He planned to give them a new beginning with a new purpose – to turn them into new people. In times of deep trouble, it may appear as though God has forgotten you, but God may preparing you, as He did the people of Judah, for a new beginning with Him at the center. Call, pray, seek, search for God will all your heart and He will be found. Believe that He wants good things for you and has a plan for your life, your family, and your business. The Christian Entrepreneur must seek God's face daily, despite any opposition. He promises the Christian Entrepreneur that he will find Him as he seeks Him diligently.

God You Said....
- And my God shall supply all your need according to His riches in glory by Christ Jesus. (*Philippians 4:19*)

The hand of God's provision is also open to us in our time of affliction. He has provided for the need of His suffering saints.

When the Christian Entrepreneur is deep in the vale of their suffering, when they have been in God's waiting room for what seems like endless days, it appears that the storehouse of God's supply is about to be exhausted. They may feel that He can do nothing more for them. But the promise of the Holy Scriptures is that He will supply all your need.

God You Said....
- You will also declare a thing, and it will be established for you; so light will shine on your ways. (*Job 22:28*)

Whatever the Christian Entrepreneur purposes in his or her strength, they shall be enabled to accomplish it. Job is letting us know that (1). God's decrees are unfrustrable, (2). His counsel shall stand, and (3). The thoughts of His heart are established to all generations.

The Christian Entrepreneur that is so guided by God will prosper and succeed in all their ways and works, to the point where whatever they are determined to do, and have a scheme formed for the execution of it, it should be brought about and confirmed.

God You Said....

- The Lord shall preserve your going out and your coming in from this time forth, and even forevermore. *(Psalm 121:8)*

Here the Psalmist was assured that God would protect him from all dangers both during the day and at night. And in case there was any room left for concern, the Psalm ends with two verses that declare the completeness of God's protection. He is the Protector over all of life, and His watchful care will last forever. Once the Christian Entrepreneur put their whole trust and confidence in God, He will be their continual portion and defense in all places, in all times, in all actions; in life, in prosperity, in adversity, in death, in time, and in eternity. Whatever you attempt will have good success.

God You Said....

- The Lord your God will make you abound in all the work of your hand, in the fruit of your body, in the increase of your livestock, and in the produce of your land for good. For the Lord will again rejoice over you for good as He rejoiced over your fathers. (*Deuteronomy 30:9*)

In every manufacture, trade, or business of life in which the Christian Entrepreneur is employed, the Lord will greatly bless them in all that they shall set their hands to in a lawful way; so that they shall abound in good things, and have enough and some to spare, a redundancy of the good things of life.

God You Said....

- The Lord will open to you His good treasure, the heavens, to give the rain to your land in its season, and to bless all the work of your hand. (*Deuteronomy 28:12*)

Here the Lord promises to open His good treasure to the Christian Entrepreneur, which is the rain. The rain is to be given in its due season, because with rain the earth is enriched. The Christian Entrepreneur has to their constant supplies (money, customers, ideas, creativity) coming from God's good treasure, and owe their obligations to Him for them (prayer, praise, worship & faith); if God withhold His rain from our businesses, the fruits of our labor will soon perish. If the Christian Entrepreneur continues to step out with faith, discipline, diligence and determination, God promises to "bless all the work of thine hand."

God You Said....

- Every place that the sole of your foot will tread upon I have given you. *(Joshua 1:3)*

Learning to mature as a Christian Entrepreneur and learning to obtain God's promises, requires a little footwork. You don't become a mature Christian Entrepreneur without walking down some difficult roads. You don't become a mature Christian Entrepreneur without facing some enemies. You don't go to bed an immature Christian Entrepreneur, and wake up the next morning having learned all the lessons you need to learn in life. God doesn't just want you lying in bed dreaming of the Promised Land, He wants you to take it. He wants you to own it. I wonder how many promises of God you have laid claim too. How many of His promises have you set your feet down on? Have you even possessed the tenth that the Israelites did?

a) ***Your foot . . . I have given you***: Entrance into the land of Canaan was entrusted to a representative. Joshua was the trustee of the land for the people. In the same way, our representative Jesus Christ goes before us and what we have in God, we possess in Him.

b) ***I have given you***: The whole land was given, but they could only posses that which they claimed (every place that the sole of your foot will tread upon I have given you). What they took must be fought for against a determined opposition. It's the same way with the Christian Entrepreneur, we must take what's ours in the marketplace.

c) God certainly could have simply eliminated all their enemies with a mere thought; but He calls Israel into partnership with Himself to see His will done. The Christian Entrepreneur is called into partnership with Jesus Christ to take dominion over the marketplace.

d) Because taking the land took effort, the challenge ahead was not for those content with Egypt, but for those who would press ahead for what God had called them to. For the Christian Entrepreneur, the challenge is not for those who have started the business, but the challenge is to those who sincerely want to bring glory to God. This is done by being committed to building multi-million dollar empires. Scripture teaches that you should leave an inheritance for your children's children.

Things To Remember

1. Expect God's best.

2. Confess God's Word daily.

3. Expect God to hear your confessions.

4. Expect positive results for your business.

5. Everyday move with a spirit of expectation.

6. Hold fast the confession of your expectation without wavering.

7. Expectation Demands Action.

8. There is a rejoicing in expectation.

Chapter 12

THE CHRISTIAN ENTREPRENEUR & WISDOM

Wisdom is the ability to see life from God's perspective and then to know the best course of action to take. Wisdom is developed through experience, insight and reflection, to discern truth and exercise good judgment. Wisdom is sometimes conceptualized as an especially well developed form of common sense. Wisdom is often considered to be a trait that can be developed by experience, but not taught.

The Christian Entrepreneur becomes wiser as he or she becomes more like Christ. We can ask for God's wisdom to guide our choices, the bible says "If you want to know what God wants you to do, ask Him, and he will gladly tell you, for He is always ready to give a bountiful supply of wisdom to all who ask Him; He will not resent it." *(James 1:5, TLB)*

God You Said....
* That their hearts may be encouraged, being knit together in love, and attaining to all riches of the full assurance of understanding, to the knowledge of the mystery of God, both of the Father and of Christ, in whom are hidden all the treasures of wisdom and knowledge. *(Colossians 2:2-3)*

Wisdom is found when you know Christ. Scripture says that wisdom is found "in Him", which means we, the Christian Entrepreneur need to get "In Him" and He In Us! Jeremiah 4:22 says, "My people are fools; they do not know Me..." There is a correlation between our relationship to the Lord and the level of wisdom we walk in! We are to know the mysteries of God! We are supposed to think like God and know Him in such a way to completely understand what He's about! That only comes when the Christian Entrepreneur truly know Him and His heart for us. Obviously, the Christian Entrepreneur will never totally understand God (Isaiah 55:9). Yet, Scripture tells us that we have the mind of Christ, that He will reveal the deep and hidden treasures to our hearts and that we can know everything He has for us (1 Corinthians 2:6-16). The more we know Jesus — His heart, His purpose, His will, His goals — the more we will make good choices. Choices are not based on feelings, desires, voices or distractions, but are based on an eternal, heavenly perspective. This then becomes a solid foundation for our spiritual growth and maturity.

God You Said....

- I will instruct you and teach you in the way you should go; I will guide you with my eye. Do not be like the horse or like the mule, which have no understanding, which must be harnessed with bit and bridle, else they will not come near you. *(Psalm 32:8-9)*

God describes some people as being like horses or mules that have to be controlled by bits and bridles. Rather than letting God guide them step by step, they stubbornly leave God only one option. If God wants to keep them useful for Him, He must use discipline and punishment. God longs to guide us with love and wisdom rather than punishment. He offers to teach us the best way to go. The Christian Entrepreneur has to accept the advice written in God's word and don't let their stubbornness keep them from obeying God.

God You Said....

- Two are better than one, because they have a good reward for their labor. For if they fall, one will lift up his companion. But woe to him who is alone when he falls, for he has no one to help him up. Again, if two lie down together, they will keep warm; but how can one be warm alone? Though one may be overpowered by another, two can withstand him. And a threefold cord is not quickly broken. *(Ecclesiastes 4:9-12)*

There are advantages to cooperating with others. Life is designed for companionship, not isolation, for intimacy, not loneliness. Some people prefer isolation, thinking they cannot trust anyone. We are not here on earth to serve ourselves, however, but to serve God and others. Don't isolate yourself and try to go it alone. Seek companions; be a team member. As an Entrepreneur, its no way possible that you can build a business alone. You're going to need help building the empire God has called you to build. Ask God to send you His choice people to work with you.

God You Said....
• A wise man will hear and increase learning, and a man of understanding will attain wise counsel. *(Proverbs 1:5)*

The wise man will never assume that he has attained perfection of knowledge; it is the fool who thinks he has attained a plateau of learning beyond which no one can teach him further. The wise man is submissive. The proud and rebellious are fools, not wise men, yet how often do we all proudly refuse counsel from others. Here the Christian Entrepreneur is told to continue to seek learning, this means reading books, attending seminars and taking entrepreneurial classes.

God You Said....
• For wisdom is better than rubies, and all the things one may desire cannot be compared with her. *(Proverbs 8:11)*

For the Christian Entrepreneur, this clearly shows the importance of knowledge of Divine truth. Gold, silver, jewels and all other forms of wealth must be left behind when this short life on earth is over, but wisdom, being an acquisition of the mind and the heart, will endure throughout all eternity. The Entrepreneur, because he is a carnal creature until he is born again, always desires things that pertain to the flesh, but these things, like the flesh, are so very temporal and fleeting. Only the soul, and what it has accumulated to itself, will last on and on and on. The Christian Entrepreneur has to continue feeding and beautifying their soul.

God You Said....

- My son, give attention to my words; Incline your ear to my sayings. Do not let them depart from your eyes; Keep them in the midst of your heart; For they are life to those who find them, And health to all their flesh. *(Proverbs 4:20-22)*

Here the Christian Entrepreneur gets a fresh call to attend to a Father's pious instructions, which is necessary to be instilled in one while he or she is still yet young in business and their character still moldable. He who refuses to hear the instruction of his Father hurts himself most of all, for in refusing to take advantage of the experience of his elders, he dooms himself to make the same business mistakes over again that the older man has already experienced. The Christian Entrepreneur is encouraged to listen and not stray away from wise instruction. Continue to seek wisdom and keep it in front of you. Wisdom brings life, blessing, honor and the favor of God.

God You Said....

- A good man deals graciously and lends; He will guide his affairs with discretion. *(Psalm 112:5)*

A good man sheweth favor, and lendeth. Having passed beyond stern integrity into open handed benevolence he looks kindly upon all around him, and finding himself in circumstances which enable him to spare a little of his wealth, he lends judiciously where a loan will be of permanent service. Providence has made him able to lend, and grace makes him willing to lend. He is not a borrower, for God has lifted him above that necessity; neither is he a hoarder, for his new nature saves him from that temptation; but he wisely uses the talents committed to him. He will guide his affairs with discretion. Those who neglect their worldly business must not plead religion as an excuse, for when a man is truly upright he exercises great care in managing his accounts, in order that he may remain so. It is sometimes hard to distinguish between indiscretion and dishonesty; carelessness in business may become almost as great an evil to others as actual knavery; a good man should not only be upright, but he should be so discreet that no one may have the slightest reason to suspect him of being otherwise. When the righteous man lends, he exercises prudence, not risking his all, for fear he should not be able to lend again, and not lending so very little that the loan is of no service. He drives his affairs, and does not allow them to drive him; his accounts are straight and clear, his plans are wisely laid, and his modes of operation carefully selected. He is prudent, thrifty, economical, sensible, judicious, discreet. The beginning of wisdom" has made him wise, the guidance of heaven has taught him to guide his affairs, and with half an eye one can see that he is a man of sound sense. Such persons greatly commend godliness. Attention to the things of heaven does not necessitate the neglect of the affairs of earth; on the contrary, he who has learned how to transact business with God ought to be best able to do business with men. The children of this world often are in their generation wiser than the children of light, but there is no reason why this proverb should continue to be true. The Christian Entrepreneur can take a lot from this passage.

God You Said....

- Thus says the Lord: "Let not the wise man glory in his wisdom, Let not the mighty man glory in his might, Nor let the rich man glory in his riches; But let him who glories glory in this, that he understands and knows Me, That I am the Lord, exercising loving kindness, judgment, and righteousness in the earth. For in these I delight," says the Lord. (*Jeremiah 9:23-24*)

The people with whom Jeremiah contended were depending on their own capabilities rather than on God. Glory here means to boast, meaning "to praise oneself." The idea is that the believer, the Christian Entrepreneur should find their real meaning and true worth in the fact that they know God and may celebrate His attributes. True knowledge of God resulting from an intimate relationship with Him will be demonstrated in the Christian Entrepreneurs character. Three attributes of God that He demands of people called by His Name are loving kindness, meaning "loyal love"; judgment, meaning "justice"; and righteousness, meaning "uprightness."

God You Said….

- Wisdom is the principal thing; therefore get wisdom. And in all your getting, get understanding. Exalt her, and she will promote you; She will bring you honor, when you embrace her. *(Proverbs 4:7-8)*

For the Christian Entrepreneur, nothing is as important as the pursuit of wisdom and understanding: with wisdom, all good things will eventually come: without it, though one may have many good things, they will eventually be lost and do no one any lasting good.

If the Christian Entrepreneur wants wisdom, he or she must decide to go after it. It takes resolve – a determination not to abandon the search once you begin no matter how difficult the road may become. This is not a once in a lifetime step, but a daily process of choosing between two paths – the wrong way and the right way. Nothing else is more important or more valuable.

Exalt her, and she shall promote you; she shall bring you honor, when you embrace her. Promotion and praise are gifts of wisdom to the Christian Entrepreneur who receives it and this promotion and praise is of the lasting kind.

God You Said….

- If any of you lacks wisdom, let him ask of God, who gives to all liberally and without reproach, and it will be given to him. But let him ask in faith, with no doubting, for he who doubts is like a wave of the sea driven and tossed by the wind. For let not that man suppose that he will receive anything from the Lord; he is a double-minded man, unstable in all his ways. *(James 1:5-8)*

The wisdom God gives is not necessarily information on how to get out of trouble, but rather insight on how to learn from one's difficulties. It is not more information about how to avoid times of testing but instead a new perspective on trials. The wisdom of God begins with a genuine reverence for the Almighty fear of the Lord and a steadfast confidence that God controls all circumstances, guiding them to His good purposes. Wisdom also means practical discernment. Again it begins with respect for God, leads to right living, and results in increased ability to tell right from wrong. God is willing to give us this wisdom, but we will be unable to receive it if our goals are self-centered instead of God-centered. To learn God's will, we need to read his Word and ask him to show us how to obey it. Then we do what he tells us.

Doubting means "to be divided in one's mind" or "to debate." The term does not describe a momentary doubt but a divided allegiance, an uncertainty.

A double-minded man is a person drawn in two opposite directions. His allegiance is divided and because of his lack of sincerity, he vacillates between belief and disbelief, sometimes thinking that God will help him and at other times giving up all hope in Him. Such a person is unstable in all his ways, not only in his prayer life. The lack of consistency in his exercise of faith betrays his general character.

God You Said....

- Give instruction to a wise man, and he will be still wiser; teach a just man, and he will increase in learning. *(Proverbs 9:9)*

There is no one so wise, but a humbled Christian Entrepreneur may gain yet more wisdom if he will heed the teachings of others. Sometimes those very new in business may bring a glorious truth to the attention of those who have been in business a long time. But learning comes only by listening. A wise Entrepreneur accepts correction and responds with gratitude to the one who points out his error. A wise person always welcomes constructive criticism, by implication, he or she is also humble. Learn from you critics; this is the path to wisdom. Wisdom begins with knowing God. He gives insight into living because He created life. To know God is not just to know the facts about Him, but to stand in awe of Him and have a relationship with Him.

God You Said....

- He who heeds the word wisely will find good, and whoever trust in the Lord, happy is he. *(Proverbs 16:20)*

Prudence in business may cause a Christian Entrepreneur to respect a person, but only by trusting in the Lord will the Christian Entrepreneur find true happiness both here and hereafter. Often in Proverbs, the exact counterpart of the different parts of the verse is not stated, but is left to be inferred. "Thus, 'He that handleth a matter (i.e., his business) wisely' needs to be supplemented by the additional thought to be conjoined with it, he must 'trust in the Lord,' not merely depend on his own sagacity, if he is both to 'find good' and be 'happy'.

The implied warning against trusting in one's own wisdom connects this with the warning against pride in verses 16:18-19. Here wisdom is the Christian Entrepreneur's true strength; and, under its guidance, he or she best accomplishes the ends of his or her being. Wisely handling the matter of his or her business gives to them the richest enjoyment. By it they will find good in the fullest sense. Without wisdom the Christian Entrepreneur will be running here and there, wasting strength which might be profitably employed. Wisdom is the compass by which the Christian Entrepreneur is to steer across the trackless waste of life; without it they are a derelict vessel.

Wisdom is never easily gained or quickly achieved; that is why a wise person increases learning. God's wisdom is a wellspring of life that can make a person happy, healthy, and alive forever. The Christian Entrepreneur can be enlightened by God's wisdom.

God You Said....
- Plans fail for lack of counsel, but with many advisers they succeed. *(Proverbs 15:22)*

When the Christian Entrepreneur makes a rash decision without properly considering proper counsel, he will have occasion to repent of his haste. "Counsel" is more commonly rendered "secret" or "secret counsel," and so seems to refer to one's inward counsel before making any decision. And it is generally wise to seek the counsel of several others who are qualified to give counsel in the particular matter to be decided.

God You Said....

- A wise man has great power, and a man of knowledge increases strength. *(Proverbs 24:5)*

Wisdom, because it is from the Lord, strengthens the Christian Entrepreneur with a mental and spiritual strength which is far more valuable than mere physical strength. Physical strength is of use only in this world, but mental and spiritual strength are of use now, and more especially in the world to come. Wisdom avails where strength cannot, for a wise man can make the strength of the mighty to work against him (Proverbs 21:22; Ecclesiastes 9:14-16).

God You Said....

- Wisdom is good with an inheritance, and profitable to those who see the sun. For wisdom is a defense as money is a defense, but the excellence of knowledge is that wisdom gives life to those who have it. *(Ecclesiastes 7:11-12)*

Here the Christian Entrepreneur is told that wisdom is protection just as money is protection. But the advantage of knowledge is that wisdom preserves the lives of its possessors. Money and prosperity can protect us from certain categories of problem, but only wisdom can preserve our lives in time. Therefore to have all the money in the world with out wisdom is empty.

God You Said....

- If the ax is dull, and one does not sharpen the edge, then he must use more strength; but wisdom brings success. *(Ecclesiastes 10:10)*

The wise person gets the job done much more quickly and efficiently than the person who is compared to a dull ax.

God You Said....

- For the Lord gives wisdom; From His mouth come knowledge and understanding; He stores up sound wisdom for the upright; He is a shield to those who walk uprightly. *(Proverbs 2:6-7)*

The Christian Entrepreneur can, by nature, get an education in worldly and human matters, but heavenly, Divine things can be understood only by the aid of the Holy Spirit, (1 Cor. 2:7-13). The Christian Entrepreneur who rejects this wisdom will be eternally unwise.

"He stores up sound wisdom for the upright; He is a shield (buckler) to those who walk uprightly." This wisdom is laid up, ready to be found upon the Christian Entrepreneur's diligence in searching for it. Note for whom this is laid up: "the righteous." This shows that God works for our good antecedent to our earliest desires for knowledge. "Buckler" means *shield*, it is certain that not only is there wisdom laid up for those who are upright, but also there is safety. If the Christian Entrepreneur depends upon God, and seek Him for wisdom, He will uphold them in their integrity and their steps will be ordered.

<u>Things To Remember</u>

1. Have the Lord "direct" your paths.

2. The Lord can help your journey in life go smoother with His blessing.

3. Give of your best to the Lord.

4. Give cheerfully and liberally, and God will empower you to give more.

5. In Christ are hidden all the treasures of wisdom and knowledge.

6. Plans fail for lack of council.

7. A man of knowledge increases strength.

8. He who heeds the word wisely will find good.

9. God will instruct you and teach you in the way you should go.

The Entrepreneurs Prayer

Father God in the Name of Jesus, you're the King of kings and Lord of lords. You're the Alpha and the Omega, You're the Beginning and the End, You're the First and the Last. The heavens and the earth all belong to You. All things are from You, through You and to You. You are my Savior, You are my Redeemer, You are my Great High Priest. You are God all by Yourself.

I come boldly to the Throne of Grace Lord, as You have commanded me, where I know I will find mercy and grace in my time of need.

I ask You to forgive me of all my sins and my faults, which have robbed me of my success in the past.

I plead the Blood of Jesus over myself to wash away all my sins and iniquities and to strengthen me.

In Jesus Name, I command my heart and mind to fear the Lord, which is the beginning of all wisdom.

In Jesus Name, I receive wisdom, and I command my heart to crave for every Word of God that comes out of the Lord's mouth.

In Jesus Name, I command my mind to be subject to the Word of God.

In Jesus Name, I purpose in my heart to walk with wise men and to flee from the companion of fools.

In Jesus Name, I purpose in my heart and mind to inquire and seek counsel from Christian business owners and Christian business leaders.

Lord, I thank you that you have anointed my life for the mission, mandate and purpose as I pursue my divine, ordained assignment. As I help others to become successful in their businesses, You in turn will help me become successful in mine.

I ask the Holy Spirit, in Jesus Name, to convict me to know that it is only by His wisdom that my business would be built.

It is only by His understanding that it will be established and only by His knowledge that my business will be filled with precious and pleasant riches.

Father, You said in Proverbs 14:23 that "In all labor there is profit, but idle chatter leads only to poverty. Father my desire is to labor for You in my business, give me the strength to accomplish what you would have me to do.

Lord, I pray this day that you would place Solomon's anointing upon me for wisdom, wealth, success and prosperity, Cyrus anointing for financial acumen, Joseph's anointing for business and economic leadership strategies, Issachar's anointing for discerning of correct times and seasons and Abraham's anointing for pioneering new territories in Jesus Name.

Lord order my steps in Your word, for Your word is a lamp to my feet and a light to my path.

I now command my heart and mind to remember that it is the Lord who gives power to get wealth, so that His Covenant can be established.

I command every spirit of fear, greed and lust of the things of the world, to get out of me in Jesus Name.

I receive the wisdom of God and knowledge and understanding that the Lord has spoken.

I command my heart in Jesus Name, to be still and know that the Lord is God.

I purpose in my heart to wait on the Lord and acknowledge Him in all decisions that I make in my business.

I curse every spirit of doubt and unbelief – I command you to get out in Jesus Name.

I curse every spirit of debt in Jesus Name.

I release by faith, in Jesus Name, wisdom, knowledge, and understanding to my family, employees and down line.

Lord give me all the right people to work with me and for me. Together we work as unto the Lord. I call forth every individual and resource assigned to assist me in the fulfillment in my Kingdom assignment.

I ask the Holy Spirit, in Jesus Name, to convict them to turn to the Lord, with all the decisions that they make regarding this business.

Open divine gates of access to a new door of opportunity; windows of divine inspiration, insight and revelation; paths of righteousness; avenues of success and prosperity; multiple streams of income and positive cash flow and highways to places of divine assignments and prosperity.

I pray that today is a day of excellence and at its conclusion I can acknowledge and be grateful for the forward motion I have made and the growth I have experienced.

Father, I speak life into my business in Jesus Name. I call things that are not as though they were.

I speak prosperity into my business in Jesus Name.

I call the money in from the North, the South, the East and the West in Jesus Name.

I call the customers in from the North, the South, the East and the West in Jesus Name.

I call the resources in from the North, the South, the East and the West in Jesus Name.

Now unto Him, who is able to do exceedingly abundantly above all that we ask or think, according to the power that works in us.

It is for these things that I pray, for I am a Christian Entrepreneur.

In Jesus Name, Amen!

PRAYER OF SALVATION

God loves you, no matter who you are, no matter what your past. God loves you so much that He gave His one and only begotten Son for you. The Bible tells us that "...whoever believes in him shall not perish but have eternal life" (John 3:16 NIV). Jesus laid down His life and rose again so that we could spend eternity with Him in heaven and experience His absolute best on earth. If you would like to receive Jesus into your life, say the following prayer out loud and mean it from your heart.

Heavenly Father, I come to You admitting that I am a sinner. Right now, I choose to turn away from sin, and I ask You to cleanse me of all unrighteousness. I believe that Your Son, Jesus, died on the cross to take away my sins. I also believe that He rose again from the dead so that I might be forgiven of my sins and made righteous through faith in Him. I call upon the name of Jesus Christ to be the Savior and Lord of my life. Jesus, I choose to follow You and ask that You fill me with the power of the Holy Spirit. I declare that right now I am a child of God. I am free from sin and full of the righteousness of God. I am saved in Jesus' name. Amen

If you prayed this prayer to receive Jesus Christ as your Savior for the first time, please contact us on the web at www.jlsministries.org to receive your free book on salvation.

Or you may write to us at:
JLS International Ministries
17207 Longleaf Drive
Bowie, MD 20716

ABOUT THE AUTHOR

Min. James L. Standfield, "*The Authority On Biblical Entrepreneurship*", is one of America's top authorities on entrepreneurship, sales, marketing, vision & goal setting. Powerfully and positively impacting audiences from around the world. James inspires entrepreneurs from all over to "raise the bar" both spiritually and professionally.

James has the gift of exaltation and throughout his life has encouraged others to fully maximize their god-given gifts, talents and abilities. He strongly believes that once you maximize these gifts, you will find true joy, happiness and peace. He strongly believes that we all can achieve our highest potential and desires to send his message to the masses.

James speaks from experience. From the trenches, he generated $1.1 million dollars in sales the very first year he was in business. He is the Founder and COO of 5 entities; Toner Express, USA, Veteran's Office Products, Lake Shore Office Products, Safe Haven Medical Supplies and The Entrepreneurial Spirit Institute. James spent 6 years in the United States Marine Corps then worked in Corporate America many years as an Auditor until the love of sales was birthed within his inner being. James found success in the sales field with Honeywell and Marriott before getting into the Office Supply Industry. After spending 2 years in the Office Supply industry as a Sales Representative, James was led by God to start his own company, Toner Express, USA . His reason for starting the company was due to customers being dissatisfied with the level of customer service and receiving faulty products.

James strength is his ability to deeply connect with audiences by sharing compelling, real-world stories that everyone can relate too. Whether it's a keynote, personal coaching, sales training, business consulting or success summit, you can count on James to exceed your expectations. His dynamic and passionate delivery creates electricity that has ignited audiences throughout the world. Trust experience. Learn from a leader. Get results with James L. Standfield, *"The Authority On Biblical Entrepreneurship"*.

To invite James L. Standfield "*The Authority On Biblical Entrepreneurship*" in to speak to your Church, Business, Organization or Multi-Level Marketing Group write to:

JLS International Ministries
17207 Longleaf Drive
Bowie, MD 20716

Or visit us on the web at
www.jlsministries.org

Or call us at 877.639.5254

*Let James come in and Inspire, Motivate,
Encourage and Challenge Your Group.*

Additional copies of this book are available from your
local bookstore or by writing:

JLS International Ministries
17207 Longleaf Drive
Bowie, MD 20716

Printed in the United States
by Baker & Taylor Publisher Services